A TRAVELER'S GUIDE TO MAKING MAGIC

About the Author

Traveling the world was always a passion of mine, stolen from carefully hoarded vacation time and extra pennies in a frugal life. After living in the Pacific Northwest for over twenty-five years, I retired from the workforce in late 2021 and moved to Portugal with my husband to create a new life. This new environment provokes and confounds me, creating opportunities to contemplate my spirituality and culture from a new vantage point.

My published books begin just after the turn of the century with *The Virtual Pagan* (2002), *CyberCoven.Org* (2004), *Magickal Connections: Creating a Healthy and Lasting Spiritual Group* (2007), and *The Virtual Pagan 2.0* (2021).

My particular passions are teaching and creating rituals. In 2000, I co-created JaguarMoon coven. Together, we teach the Art of Ritual class, a year-long "witchcraft 101" course taught in an inclusive coven setting. Class and coven celebrate the seasons, work magick, and share the mysteries in a unique, mentor-based framework. Information about the class and coven is at www.jaguarmoon.org.

After coordinating the Review Circle for The Beltane Papers magazine for seven years, I used that as a model to create Facing North: A Community Resource in 2006.[1] There, my Review Circle and I have published hundreds of reviews of items we think the Pagan/Alternative Spiritual community would find interesting.

I can always be found at www.lisamcsherry.com.

---

1 Lisa Mc. Sherry, *Facing North.* Available: www.facingnorth.net.

A TRAVELER'S GUIDE TO MAKING MAGIC

LISA MCSHERRY

Chicago, IL

Paperback ISBN: 978-1-964537-46-7
Library of Congress Control Number on file.

Published by:
Crossed Crow Books, LLC
518 Davis St, Suite 205
Evanston, IL 60201
www.crossedcrowbooks.com

Printed in the United States of America.
IBI

Also: awesome that you've read so much of this fine print! Most people skip this part, thinking it's boring. But for you, the thorough reader, I offer a collection of unusual words that you will not find elsewhere in this book. *Apricate, Erinaceous, Perspicacious,* and *Zeugma.* Excellent words for an excellent person!

Other Books by Lisa McSherry

A Witch's Guide to Crafting Your Practice: Create a Magical Path that Works for You

The Virtual Pagan 2.0

Magickal Connections: Creating a Lasting and Healthy Spiritual Group

Acknowledgments

No writer ever does it alone. I have enjoyed tremendous and constant support while creating this book.

Christy Mann gave me direct, specific guidance that got this project out of shopping mode. Blake Malliway, Emma Kowalczyk, and Gabriella De La Hoya have been champions, breathing new life into this project just when it was at its nadir. And a special thank you to Jason Mankey and Aaron Leitch for answering obscure questions with grace, humor, and a pile of new reading!

To all members of JaguarMoon Coven, past, present, and future: I could not do this without you. You are the Wheel that moves me forward in Service.

Always and forever, John. My first reader and constant sounding board, my best friend, and the rock of stability within the grand adventure of my life.

Sempre, meu amor.

Contents

INTRODUCTION

Until late 2021, I owned a spacious home brimming with magical items. Protective wards discreetly adorned each doorway, ensuring that our sanctuary remained secure. Baskets were filled with wild-harvested seed pods, lichen, and trinkets nestled within cupboards, while aromatic herbs dangled in bundles, air-drying to perfection. Within my workspace, a capacious closet boasted shelves adorned with an assortment of candles, incense, oils, and an array of stones. Whether conjuring spells or engaging in sacred rituals, I could seamlessly immerse myself with little need for elaborate preparations.

Looking back, I realize that my meticulous—perhaps even excessive—organization acted as a coping mechanism. My life was incredibly hectic, demanding the level of preparedness and organization I maintained. Prior to the COVID-19 pandemic (March 2020, for readers in the distant future), my typical day consisted of rushing home from a grueling twelve-hour shift just in time to lead a ritual with JaguarMoon, the coven I helped found in 2000. Even after the world was locked down, although my commute vanished, my life remained overflowing with responsibilities. I know I wasn't alone in this quest for busyness and the need for everything to be "just so." I see now that it was an attempt to exert a sense of control over at least one aspect of my life, as other areas often felt chaotic and beyond my grasp. Ensuring I had all the necessary tools for spellwork became a necessity, as there was rarely any time to search for items at the last minute.

In 2021, my husband and I made a life-altering choice that would forever change our paths: we decided to retire from our careers, sell our home (along with nearly all its contents), and embark on a new adventure in Portugal. The longing to explore more of Europe had always been within us, and we began receiving unmistakable signs that, as a famous saying goes, tomorrow is not promised to anyone. Waiting any longer could mean forfeiting our dreams. Once the decision was solidified, it took us approximately five months of intense decluttering and letting go. We sold, gave away, or donated everything that wasn't essential or deeply cherished. The process of purging brought about a mixture of liberation and trepidation, and I'm still navigating the effects it had on my psyche.

After we moved, I lived for almost a year without a formal altar and essentially no magical tools. During that year, my spiritual practice became one of the bare necessities as I redefined what was vital for me to work magic and saw why some of the "extra" things are valuable, while others are just plain extra. Leaving my now practically empty nest and traveling elsewhere for sightseeing brought home what I was missing on the road and things I didn't think twice about anymore.

With the transition to our new home complete, I find myself with more time on my hands. However, I am still adjusting to the challenge of working with limited supplies, as the abundance I once had is no longer at my disposal. Although the city where I reside offers a plentiful selection of incense and candles, procuring herbs beyond the culinary variety and ethically sourced stones proves to be considerably more challenging. Acquiring English-language books requires ordering and shipping them from outside the country, and browsing and handling Tarot decks at a local bookstore before making a purchase is rarely ever an option.

More importantly, I now travel a lot, much more than I ever did before. Short trips, long trips. In-country and all over the European Union and the United States. Renting cars, riding trains, flying in planes, and even floating in ferries and other boats. With this increased opportunity has come a growing thoughtfulness in choosing where I travel and why.

When I began to indulge my travel itch almost twenty years ago, I followed the typical tourist's well-trod path (and, of course, there is nothing wrong with going to popular places—they're famous for a reason). I went to the Tower of London, took pictures of the Louvre's Pyramid, woke up at the crack of dawn to get an early look at the Vatican's art collection, and on and on. However, as I've grown and experienced more things, I've realized that traveling offers more than just "postcard possibilities"; there are also incredible opportunities to deepen my understanding of my magical practice.

Like many eclectic Pagans, I have come to honor many aspects of the gods from a diverse roster of cultures and periods of history, seeing other parts of the world has allowed me to become more grounded in my understanding of those cultures and deities. Throughout these many journeys, I continue to teach classes, offer workshops, talk on podcasts, celebrate esbats, and honor the seasons at sabbats. Part of what I've learned in all this is that my travel doesn't have to interfere with my magical life; in fact, that part of my life is more robust than ever.

Thus, we now find ourselves with this book. While some of what I've discovered has been intensely personal, my travel life has taught and continues to teach me many things that would benefit practically everyone, and you'll benefit from these lessons without quite so many of the "hard way" varieties. Regardless of whether you take a simple visit to a local park or embark on a grand world tour, the practice of magic can be seamlessly integrated into every aspect of your journey. This book serves as a comprehensive guide, offering a wealth of ideas for incorporating magic into your travels—whether it involves protecting yourself, facilitating a smooth passage, or simply staying attuned to the rhythms of the seasons.

Nevertheless, it's important to note that this book does not offer a definitive roadmap to the "One True Way." In fact, it takes quite the opposite approach. Consider me a companion on your journey, guiding you to navigate around potential obstacles and highlighting what appears to be the most promising route. However, it is you who holds the power to provide context and establish the framework for the practices I explore. It's worth emphasizing that very few aspects of what I present require strict adherence to my instructions. This book serves as a guidebook, rather than a rigid rule book, allowing you the freedom to adapt and personalize the practices to suit your unique path.

Within the pages of *A Traveler's Guide to Making Magic,* I will delve into the realm of magic, which I perceive as a spiritual practice rooted in transformation, awareness, and responsibility. Each of us is a divine and powerful being capable of altering reality through the focused application of energy, a pursuit that we refer to as "magic."

Magic is a natural and neutral force accessible to all, and I firmly believe that assuming responsibility for the consequences of our actions is an essential aspect of working magic. Engaging in the process of magic involves delving into our own will and desires, discerning and removing that which is unwanted, unhealthy, or superfluous, so as to effect practical change in our lives. In this endeavor, we align ourselves with the natural world and tap into the abundant energy that permeates nature. Many practitioners of this spiritual path identify as Witches. Similar to how swimming enables us to navigate through deep pools of water with ease, aligning our energies with the larger reality enhances our ability to bring about practical transformations.

However, it's worth noting that one does not need to adhere to a specific belief in any deity to derive significant value from this book. If you are new to magic or desire insight into how I define and engage with it, I recommend referring to Chapter One: Basic Magic.

Spirituality outside of mainstream religions exhibit an immense diversity, and it is important to recognize that counterexamples can easily be found for any general statement I make. It is crucial to note that the Witchcraft I personally engage with is deeply rooted in my European and American lineages, reflecting the primary cultures of my teachers, family, and students. It is essential to acknowledge that perceptions of Paganism, Witchcraft, and Witches vary significantly across non-European cultures. Even within Europe, substantial regional differences exist. These observations emphasize the fact that, while my language may occasionally present ideas with a sense of absolute accuracy, it is vital to interpret them as generalizations rather than absolutes. Adding a note stating, "Of course, this does not hold true for every single culture; be sure to consult your own references according to your comfort" after every paragraph would become cumbersome for all parties involved, so please presume it is there.

Indeed, it is true that practicing magic or identifying as a Witch is not a prerequisite for utilizing this book. Although having a basic understanding of magic may enable you to grasp certain concepts more readily, the fundamental techniques shared within its pages may prove to be more familiar and accessible than you might anticipate. Even if you have never regarded yourself as a practitioner of magic, if you are acquainted with cultural phenomena such as "visualizing your desires to manifest them," prayer, or making a wish on a birthday candle or the first star of the evening, you will find the energetic practices I call "magic" are familiar.

Walking Lightly on the Earth

I would be remiss if I didn't acknowledge that travel has complex ethical and environmental problems. Those of us in Western nations enjoy vast wealth and privilege relative to much of the rest of the world. Ethical travel is often presented to us as straightforward; offsetting our carbon footprint through financial contributions or opting not to have our towels washed daily. However, it is crucial to recognize that in many of the breathtaking (developing) countries we visit, the local communities rely on tourism as a vital source of economic support. Unfortunately, if we are not conscientious, this reliance on tourism can lead to detrimental environmental consequences.

"Greenwashing" refers to the deceptive practice of companies portraying themselves as environmentally sustainable while failing to follow through on their claims or engaging in superficial actions that offer little to no real benefit (or may even be harmful). One example often highlighted is the promotion of reduced (at-our-request) towel-washing practices by hotels as a sustainable measure. This practice, though helpful to some extent, does not warrant the exaggerated attention it often receives. Yes, it saves energy and water, but it also saves the companies money. Furthermore, it raises questions about the methods used for washing and the chemical products involved in the process. Similarly, promoting the use of recycled paper is not inherently negative, but a significant portion of the paper we currently utilize comes from sustainably managed tree farms where trees are specifically cultivated and replanted for future harvesting, rather than clearing precious natural forests like the Amazon.

The ethical issues prevalent in tourism are horrifying:

- **Income Distribution:** While tourism is a massive global industry, it does not always result in substantial economic benefits for local communities. In many places, large multinational companies dominate the local economy as employers and buyers, overshadowing local providers. Yet, the jobs provided offer low wages and limited benefits, and a significant portion of the income generated often flows into the coffers of large (Western) corporations, rather than directly benefiting local economies. Compare the impact of expansive, all-inclusive resorts to locally owned accommodations to illustrate this point.
- **Exploitation:** As with many issues, women and children are among the most vulnerable groups disproportionately affected by the negative consequences of tourism. From young children engaged in street vending to young women facing gender-based pay disparities in the industry, the harmful impact extends across various aspects. It is crucial to acknowledge the pervasive existence of the vast multi-million-dollar sex trade that exploits individuals within the tourism context.
- **Animal Welfare:** Let's be honest—wild animals do not want to be put on display, and their offspring do not seek cuddling from humans. We don't need scientific studies to show us that the dolphin performing in a show or the elephant being ridden isn't genuinely enjoying these activities. Although there are forms of tourism that aim to support animal conservation, it would be naive to assume that this is the prevailing norm.

As travelers, we can feel helpless and ill-informed, lacking sufficient information to determine whether our money contributes to genuinely sustainable practices. It is often entirely opaque as to whether a company's commitment to promoting diversity, actual environmental impact, or the extent to which they positively impact their communities is real, rather than an advertisement. Finding this information requires going beyond surface-level assessments and engaging in deeper exploration to truly understand the values and actions of the businesses we choose to support during our travels.

One way to address our need for better information is to seek out certifications and information from reputable research organizations and companies. These places offer indicators of a company's commitment to responsible practices and provide valuable insights into their ethical standards. By prioritizing certified businesses, we can make more informed choices that align with our values and support organizations dedicated to promoting sustainable and responsible tourism. The ones I am aware of are:

- BCorp[1]
- Earthcheck[2]
- The Conscious Travel Foundation[3]

I strongly encourage you to take the initiative to educate yourself about the multifaceted and ever-evolving issues surrounding sustainable and ethical tourism. By delving into these topics, you will gain a deeper understanding of the challenges at hand and be better equipped to make informed decisions as a responsible traveler. Stay informed, engage with reliable sources, and actively seek out opportunities to contribute positively to the global travel landscape. Some places to start learning include:

- United Nations Global Code of Ethics for Tourism[4]
- World Committee on Tourism Ethics (ECTE), Tips for Responsible Traveler[5]

---

1 B Corporation, *B Lab Global,* 2025. bcorporation.net.

2 EarthCheck, *EarthCheck,* 2024. earthcheck.org.

3 The Conscious Travel Foundation, *The Conscious Travel Foundation,* ÀNI Private Resorts, Joro Experiences, 2024. theconscioustravelfoundation.com.

4 United Nations, "Global Code of Ethics for Tourism," *UN Tourism,* United Nations, Aug. 2020. Available: www.unwto.org/background-global-code-ethics-tourism.

5 United Nations, "World Committee on Tourism Ethics," United Nations. www.unwto.org/world-committee-tourism-ethics%20.

- Tearfund, Ethical Practice and Sustainability[6]
- Conservation International, Code of Ethics[7]
- United Nations Environment Programme (UNEP), Environmental Codes of Conduct for Tourism[8]
- World Wildlife Fund (WWF), Values in Action: WWF's Core Standards of Performance[9]
- United Nations World Tourism Organization (UNWTO), Sustainable Development[10]

Amidst the challenges, there is indeed some positive news to embrace. The global pandemic that unfolded in 2020 and beyond caused significant disruptions to the tourism industry, sparking a vital conversation about the importance of conservation and preservation in travel. As a result, sustainable practices are gaining momentum and becoming more widespread. With increased attention and resources dedicated to sustainability, travel experiences are becoming more enjoyable and rewarding.

One way we can contribute is by supporting agritourism, which directly bolsters local businesses and channels resources beyond urban areas. Engaging in volunteer work that benefits communities is another impactful way to make a difference. Additionally, there is a growing trend toward eco- and cultural tourism, allowing us to immerse ourselves in the authentic experiences of a region rather than merely passing through as casual visitors. These shifts enable us to connect more deeply with the places we explore and foster a greater appreciation for their ecological and cultural richness.

---

6 Tearfund, "Ethical Practice and Sustainability," *Tearfund*, The Evangelical Alliance Relief Fund. Available: www.tearfund.org.nz/Ethical-Practice-and-Sustainability.

7 Conservation International, "Code of Ethics," *Conservation International*, 2025. Available: www.conservation.org/about/our-policies/code-of-ethics%20.

8 United States Environment Programme: Industry and Environment. "Environmental Codes of Conduct for Tourism." (UNEP, 1995).

9 WWF. *World Wildlife Fund.* "Values in Action: WWF's Core Standards of Performance." wwf.panda.org/discover/about_wwf/our_values/?.

10 United Nations. *UN Tourism.* "Sustainable Development." www.unwto.org/sustainable-development.

Moreover, small steps you can take will always make a positive difference:

1. **Turn off the power when you aren't using it.** A notable practice observed in many European hotel rooms is the requirement to insert your key card to activate electricity, which serves as a beneficial habit to adopt. Avoid leaving the air conditioning running when you are not in the room and charge your electronics only when necessary. You might also consider unplugging unused items to conserve energy. These small actions contribute to reducing energy consumption and promoting sustainable habits during your stay.
2. **Eliminate the disposables.** Although it can be challenging when "on the run," consider ways to eliminate or minimize single-use waste (especially plastic). One approach is to carry a reusable set of a stainless-steel water bottle, utensil set, and straw. Easy to clean and lightweight, this set greatly reduces disposables. If you add a cloth napkin, you eliminate more disposables. I am a big fan of travel-size containers of the various items we need for hygiene and always look for refillable options.
3. **Be conscious of your waste.** In many establishments catering to travelers, food is often served generously. Consider ordering less than your usual portion size or sharing plates. Doing so helps reduce food waste with a bonus of being able to try new foods while not overwhelming your appetite.
4. **Don't litter.** It may seem like an obvious reminder, but unfortunately, I've come across numerous places during my travels that were marred by piles of waste left behind by previous visitors. It is truly disheartening and, frankly, quite rude. So, please make sure to pack out your garbage or use the available bins. Even better, if you spot litter while you're leaving, consider taking some of it with you to help keep the area clean. Let's all do our part to preserve the beauty of our surroundings and show respect for the places we visit.
5. **Be courteous to nature.** By this, I mean stay on the path, no matter how the wild beckons. Also, don't feed, touch, or scare

wildlife. Worse than scaring wildlife, sometimes too much interaction with humans can teach animals that human predators aren't dangerous. Never *ever* touch the coral.

6. **Avoid flying as much as possible.** Airplanes are fast and efficient, but their carbon footprint is about one hundred times that of a bus or train. Even so, I recognize that some places can't be reached otherwise, or the time is prohibitive. This is another place where I am counseling you to make the best decisions you can, not absolutism.
7. **Walk or utilize local metro services rather than hiring a car.** While major cities like London and Paris are renowned for their exceptional underground railway systems, it's worth noting that many other cities boast reliable bus services or light rail networks. Just because you may not have heard about them doesn't mean they don't exist. It's always advisable to check ahead and explore these local transportation options. Mixing with the locals and embracing the ride can offer unique experiences and insights. Sometimes, public transport in certain regions may appear unconventional or unfamiliar. Take, for example, the Philippines' "jeepney," a vibrant and elaborately adorned micro-bus/taxi hybrid. If you've never encountered one, it can be quite surprising. During such moments, my husband adopts a mantra: "Millions of people do this daily; it must work." This perspective helps maintain patience and an open mind when encountering new foods or experiences that may initially seem out of the ordinary.

For those of us identifying outside of mainstream religions, our focus lies in actively seeking sustainable solutions and adopting a mindful approach to travel, minimizing our impact as much as possible. The initial and essential step is to cultivate a heightened awareness of our surroundings, enabling us to discern where and how we can effectively channel our magical practices. It is crucial to emphasize that this perspective is not intended to scold or create an awkward dichotomy. We acknowledge that individuals relying on employment within large multinational hotels or the restaurant industry play vital roles in these complex ecosystems. From the hardworking front-line employees to the intricate network of food purveyors and support services, the industry encompasses various stakeholders. By recognizing this interconnectedness, we can navigate our magical journeys with intention while remaining mindful of the broader context in which we operate.

Just over a decade ago, the landscape of travel looked markedly different. It was primarily characterized by local excursions, often undertaken by car, to familiar destinations that families would visit repeatedly, often on an annual basis. A classic example is the family camping trip or summer vacation to the same lake or campground. International travel was a sporadic luxury, evoking a sense of excitement as travelers were bid farewell by their loved ones at the airport, only to return with cherished souvenirs, captivating stories, and photographs. Discussions surrounding over-tourism were not as prevalent, as it was not a prominent concern at the time. While destinations certainly appreciate the economic benefits derived from tourism, it is crucial not to overlook the potential damage that can be inflicted as a result of our actions as travelers. The impacts we can have on the places we visit should not be taken lightly or dismissed.

There are numerous ways to ensure that our visit makes a positive contribution while minimizing any negative impact we may have.

First and foremost, let's *prioritize supporting local businesses.* Steer clear of large tour groups, agencies, and cruise ships. While a cruise may promise exotic destinations, a significant portion of the spending remains with the cruise operators, often resulting in detrimental effects on the environment and local infrastructure. Instead, seek out local guides who can offer insightful tours and help you engage respectfully in cultural activities.

A very early visit to the Sistine Chapel is a special memory because our small group had it to ourselves for almost half an hour. Later in the day, large groups were herded through and anyone stopping had to deal with one of the carabinieri in charge of crowd control shooing them along.

Another strategy is to extend our stay in centrally located lodging. By immersing ourselves in one place for a longer period, we can savor a slower and more thoughtful pace. We can explore attractions when the crowds are fewer, allowing us to truly enjoy the experience with a calm and relaxed mindset. Embracing the rhythm of the locals, we can shop at local markets, prepare our meals, and witness the vibrant nightlife from the cozy corner cafés. Staying in locally supported accommodations not only fosters a sense of connection, but also minimizes disruption for the local community. Traditional lodgings such as hotels, hostels, and bed and breakfast establishments are often situated in designated tourism zones, aiding a harmonious coexistence with the locals.

To show respect for locals, make a concerted effort to adhere to local rules and regulations. Prioritize researching and familiarizing yourself with the specific guidelines before your trip. Illegally parked vehicles have become a significant issue in small communities worldwide. In Europe, there are designated times for vehicle access, often restricted for deliveries or reserved for overnight parking by residents. While mistakes can happen, strive to be informed rather than ignorant. This principle extends to items such as drones and selfie sticks, which may seem like exciting innovations for enhancing your travel experience. However, due to their excessive presence, popular destinations have had to impose regulations to mitigate their disruptive impact. By being considerate and mindful of these restrictions, we can contribute to a more harmonious and respectful environment for both locals and fellow travelers.

We can use public transport as much as possible, *but not at rush hour.* Tram #28 in Lisbon, with its charming vintage cars and route encompassing prominent landmarks, is a popular choice for tourists. However, locals have abandoned it due to long lines primarily consisting of tourists. In Venice, Line A offers a splendid opportunity to explore the entire city via waterways, functioning as a regular bus route. Paying heed to the designated local usage times will help you steer clear of crowded situations, reduce the risk of pickpocketing, and foster a more harmonious coexistence with the local community.

Siena, Italy, is a walled town with parking outside its walls. Our mapping program took us inside the walls, but the parking lot was on the other side, and there were other vehicles around us, so we trusted it up a narrowing street, then through an arch (still with other cars around), followed by a left down a very narrow passage just wide enough for the car. This was typical for Italian hill towns, and we could see that it opened up just ahead. "That must be the way to the outside, and parking is just a bit after that," I said as we drove out onto Il Campo. You know, the place where they hold the annual horse race, the main public space and historic center of Siena, one of Europe's greatest medieval squares...and 100% not a road. We stopped dead and had a moment of panic. Looking around, I spotted an alley wide enough for us to fit through just to the left, and we quickly took that exit before anyone could yell at us.

While seeking unique and captivating photo opportunities is undeniably exciting, it is imperative to respect the environment. Ecosystems are delicate and easily strained by tourism, often lacking sufficient time to recover. Recognized attractions such as Reykjadalur in Iceland and Maya Bay in Thailand (also known as James Bond Island) have been closed to tourism to allow them the chance to rejuvenate. Just as I mentioned earlier about seashells and rocks, refrain from altering natural elements you encounter, no matter how enticing it may be. Avoid leaving your mark, whether it's through attaching locks to bridges or carving names into trees. Instead, actively seek ways to support the ecosystem, such as using reef-safe sunscreen even when it is not obligatory. By deeply respecting the environment, we can contribute to the preservation and flourishing of the remarkable landscapes we have the privilege to explore.

In addition to honoring the environment, it is essential to respect the local culture. Exploring different cultures is often a primary motivation for travel, but the immersive experience can sometimes feel overwhelming. Allow yourself moments of comfort and familiarity amidst the unfamiliarity, ensuring that not every minute is filled with novelty. Not every place we explore has to feel like "home." Resist the urge to recreate your home environment in every place you visit.

One of the most enchanting places I've ever experienced, both artistically and spiritually, is the Garden of Cosmic Speculation. Situated in Dumfriesshire, Scotland, this private residence belongs to Charles Jencks, an esteemed artist and landscape architect. Jencks has transformed vast expanses of land into captivating art spaces. Although he desired to share his home with visitors, the delicate ecosystem could not withstand constant foot traffic. As a solution, he opened his home to the public for one day each year as part of the Garden Scheme in Scotland. Despite Jencks' passing in 2019, his home remains a cherished component of the scheme, allowing future generations to appreciate its beauty.

Embrace the unique essence of each destination, cherishing the opportunity to immerse yourself in new and enriching cultural experiences. I find myself enjoying local culture the most when I do three things:

- Indulging in local cuisine is an integral part of my travel exploration, but I've learned to be mindful of my own preferences. While I'm open to culinary adventures, Anthony Bourdain I am not (while I may eagerly savor every variety of seafood available, I draw the line at insects—they're a firm "never, no-how, no-way" for me). So, I make a point of researching local food options and customs beforehand. By understanding the local food culture in advance, I can embark on my culinary explorations with confidence and enjoyment.
- By learning some of the language, I immerse myself in the local culture. Each culture has its own customs and greetings. For instance, in Portugal, it's customary to greet the person behind the counter before shopping in small shops and bodegas, although this custom may not extend to larger stores and malls. In Greece, locals say "*yassas*" ("hello") to one another instead of "*kalimera*" ("good morning"). By acquiring a few phrases and understanding their appropriate usage, you demonstrate to the locals that you value and respect their culture. Going beyond the usual "where is the bathroom?" and being able to ask about someone's day can create meaningful connections. Countless encounters with locals have transformed from mere "professional exchanges" to genuine human experiences through the power of language and genuine interest.
- I familiarize myself with local etiquette to navigate cultural norms with ease. Understanding what to wear and when, as well as how to behave in restaurants (not just how to eat, but also norms for speaking loudly, gesturing widely, and so forth), provides valuable insights into local traditions. For instance, religious sites often have guidelines regarding the covering of heads, shoulders, and knees. Respecting these guidelines demonstrates reverence rather than feigning belief. Additionally, in certain countries, eating with the left hand is considered impolite. Prior research on these cultural nuances ensures a more enjoyable and respectful travel experience. By embracing local etiquette, we show consideration for the customs of the places.

As always, stay conscious of your choices to create a positive dynamic. You aren't just improving the experience of the local people; by syncing yourself with the culture you're visiting, you are making it easier for you to get the most from the experience. By implementing these approaches, we can actively contribute to the well-being of the places we visit while fostering a more meaningful and authentic travel experience.

How To Use This Book

Travel is an adventure, but it is also a discombobulating experience. Moreover, what you're going to need as you prepare will be different from what someone else needs, and what you need on your next trip is likely to be different from what you'll need in a few years. As such, there's no reason to think that all portions of this book will always be equally valuable to you. While I (naturally) think everything contained within is useful, that doesn't mean all of it is on point every time you travel. A read-through—or at least a skim—of the entire book is probably wise, since sometimes you don't even know that you need a piece of advice until you read it. After that, however, I'd consider *A Traveler's Guide to Making Magic* more of a reference book than a narrative work. There's a lot of good information in Chapter Six: Magic by Location, but once you know it's there, you'll probably only go to the parts of that chapter that deal with the kinds of places you're about to travel.

When considering magical options for an upcoming trip, you'll want to consider Chapter Seven: Specific Spells and Charms. For best results when using those spells, cross-reference them with Chapter Two: Correspondences. On the other hand, reading about ethical considerations in traveling is the kind of thing that, once absorbed, may only ask for a refresher occasionally. Based on the state of my travel notes over the years, I imagine that a happy owner of this book will be someone who has extensively used sticky notes or the excerpts feature on your e-reader. Barring all that, dog-ear many pages (be still, my book-loving heart).

A Traveler's Guide can also be used in the opposite direction, in a manner of speaking. I would not be surprised if, as you read about the preparations you can make for different circumstances, a new idea for a trip sparks in your mind. I'd almost be disappointed if my suggestions for marrying your vacation travel with opportunities for spiritual growth didn't get you thinking about new destinations and new focuses for upcoming journeys. What sparks an idea will be different for everyone.

If you harbor (ha) a fear of boats, exploring the realm of travel-by-water protective charms could provide an unanticipated source of solace, igniting thoughts of the picturesque San Juan Islands in the Puget Sound. Delving into the origins of your patron deity might soon beckon you to embark on a pilgrimage to their ancient temple in Turkey. Inspiration has a delightful way of catching us off guard, rendering it impossible to pinpoint which chapter will set your imagination ablaze. This very paragraph might set off a cascade of tangential musings that culminate in an impromptu journey to Tokyo. Within the pages of this book lies a hidden kernel of an idea for a remarkable trip you never imagined taking.

In addition to the emotional turmoil of preparing, packing, and leaving for a journey, traveling is fraught with insecurity, the unfamiliar, and potential impediments, producing a certain amount of anxiety. Of course, the same can be said about life itself! Travel is an ancient and universal metaphor for life—a path, a road, a voyage, a journey, a trip. Because of travel's uncertainty and potential perils, people everywhere have always petitioned the Powers That Be for protection and smooth passage.

A Benediction as You Begin

The same concepts and practices for creating a sacred space in your home also apply to making temporary domiciles. It may help you to think of your stops along the road simply as outposts of your home base. For all the advice I've provided here, I would not suggest that you take up all-new practices simply because you're traveling. Instead, what

I hope I've provided in the coming pages are methods for adapting your spiritual life so that it comes with you wherever you go. With the freedom from being untethered, you can explore your world, whether down the road or across the vast seas. This exploration can then let you deepen your connection to your spiritual practice, or perhaps even discover new practices altogether.

I'll end our beginning with a variation of a blessing used in my house since childhood:

May the road rise to meet you
May the wind be always at your back
May the sun shine warm upon your face
May the rain fall gently upon your fields.
And until we meet again,
May the All hold you in the palm of its hand.

—Lisa
Northern Portugal, 2025

We are all visitors to this time, this place.
We are just passing through.
Our purpose here is to observe, to learn, to grow, to love
...and then we return home.

—Australian Aboriginal Proverb

Chapter One
Basic Magic

If we are going to talk about magic, let's avoid confusion by starting with a common language. After all, there are many kinds of magic in the world, from formal ceremonial magic that channels power through precise incantations to cultural inheritances in which nothing has ever been set down in writing. The simplest "I wish that…" is a form of magic.

If you are entirely new to the idea of working magic, it can feel a bit scary. Your practice may have led you to these things already, but let's ensure we are all on the same page (if you'll excuse the pun). If you are an experienced practitioner, I expect you can skim these pages very quickly to note any irregularities compared to your practice; then again, a little refresher never hurts anybody.

Some spell it *magick* to emphasize the difference between stage or illusion magic and the process of effecting change. Throughout my long writing career, I've used both.

Alternative spirituality is primarily defined as not being an organized religion, and many call themselves Pagan (from the Latin *paganus,* meaning "a person from the country") to indicate their status as outside the mainstream, or Abrahamic, traditions. Pagan is an umbrella term and includes all spiritual paths influenced by the pre-Christian beliefs in Europe and adjacent areas of North Africa and the Near East. Similarly, some folk in our wide umbrella of "alternative" spirituality prefer the term Heathen, from the Old English *hæthen* of Germanic origin, related to Dutch *heiden* and German *heide;* generally regarded as a specifically Christian use of a Germanic adjective meaning "inhabiting open country," from the base of *heath.*[11] Many who embrace this term show an interest in rural, low-impact,

11 Oxford English Dictionary (Oxford University Press, 2023).

or off-the-grid living. Of course, many from other paths also embrace these ideas and ideals, as Paganism as an umbrella term encompasses many ways of life, beliefs, and cultural practices.

In general, Pagans celebrate life and follow practices that encourage their practitioners to align their energy with that found in the natural world. They also usually have moral and ethical precepts that require developing a strong sense of personal responsibility for their actions, a practice that includes the worship of one of more deities and promoting their own and the community's success.[12] One of the most common terms used is Witchcraft. My unique journey follows the path of a Witch, and I sincerely hope that the mention of this term doesn't deter you from continuing to explore the contents of this book. In my mind, Witchcraft offers a genuinely eclectic and varied collection of spiritual practices that can be adapted infinitely to our own needs and the challenges our lives bring us.

At the core, even as a newcomer, trust your instincts. Question everything—even what I am saying—and compare it to your feelings. It's difficult to do; we're conditioned to only rely on knowledge and logic, ignoring our feelings as untrustworthy. However, the more you follow your instincts, the easier and more reliable your choices will be.

Magic itself is a tool, neutral in existence. Like any tool, it can help or harm, and the choice is in the hands of the wielder. In practice, however, we can generalize performing magic as having four steps.

In my model of how magic works, I recognize four main steps. They are:

1. Intent
2. Creation
3. Raising
4. Sending

Let's look at each of these in turn.

---

12 I recommend my book, *A Witch's Guide to Crafting Your Practice,* if you are very new to magic. It offers clear directions on how to successfully start and build a spiritual practice based on your needs.

Intention Is the Start

The first step in doing magic is always the decision to do magic. That may sound ridiculously simplistic, but examine the difference between "this spell I read about might be just the thing I need" and "I've got the spell I need; I'll do it at the next waxing moon." Certainty of purpose is the foundation upon which successful magic is built. Once you are sure that magic is the answer you're looking for, it is then critical that you formulate your spell or ritual as precisely and clearly as possible so as to do exactly what it is that you want to accomplish—no more and no less.

Never assume that your intent is clear or that the powers you are petitioning will understand what you mean. Some believe that magic (or the powers that manipulate it) have a mischievous streak to them and, like the genie in many old stories, will actively look for a way to twist your words. Others see magic as an unthinking energy pool that can make no deductions and must, therefore, be directed with excruciating detail. In my experience, it's something in between, less mischievous and wiser. Many views on magic exist, but few (if any) see magic as an intuitive or empathic force that can take a hint, so to speak, not out of unkindness so much as any source of magic would be so different from the human experience that it wouldn't have any reason to intuit our thoughts.

I find that writing out my intentions, then saying them out loud and examining my words, while hearing them helps clarify what I am trying to achieve while also "catching out" unintended ambiguity. It's not that writing in and of itself is somehow magical, nor is hearing my words said aloud, so much as the process of doing so illuminates my intent and helps me focus on what I truly want.

We had a critical delay at the exact worst moment. My husband and I were at the end of a long day of travel; we left Nantes, France, in the morning, driving our rental car several hours back to the airport near Paris. Dropping the car was no problem, and we reached our gate with plenty of time to spare. Unfortunately, the plane ended up leaving late, and not just a wee bit. We sat at the gate for almost two hours while a system upgrade was implemented at our arrival airport. This meant we would arrive very close to our last connection, just a little hop up the coast to Porto. It was the end of a very long day, and I just wanted to get into bed. So, I worked a little magic, visualizing climbing into bed and getting to sleep.

Can you spot the problem? I knew what I was thinking, but my intention needed to be clearer; chalk it up to road weariness. I forgot to say anything about it being my bed I climbed into that night. Sure enough, we were told at the gate that we hadn't missed our connecting flight because it had been canceled and was rescheduled for the next morning. That said, the universe (in my worldview) has a sense of humor, and we were given a hotel room for the night. Nice, except that our new flight was leaving in less than five hours. I slept about an hour in that bed. I got what I asked for, but it wasn't what I wanted.

Creating Your Magic

Once you are clear about what you want, the next step is to prepare the magic. Whether working a spell or creating a charm, developing an elaborate ritual space or making it up on the fly, this is where the practice and the craft aspects of Witchcraft come into play. Even the simplest spur-of-the-moment spell will benefit from taking a moment to consider what you will do. Creating your magic will also be a last double-check on your intentions. As you set the concrete steps that you will be taking, it is another chance to notice whether those steps align with what you told yourself you were setting out to do. Whatever your practice calls for, choose what tools you will use and what forms your magic will take. If I'm at home, that means changing my altar to reflect my intention and getting my essential tools in place. I take time to clean everything as a sign of respect. As I craft my spell, I'll include specific things on hand, like types of stone or the smell of the incense I'm using. "What about when I'm not at home and don't have access to my usual implements," you ask? We'll look at that in Chapter Four: Tools for the Journey.

I strongly advocate developing a personal collection of symbolic language called correspondences. Using the principles of "As Above, So Below," we harness these symbols' energies to access the universe's endless power. For example, when we pass a carefully selected stone through the smoke of a specifically chosen incense, we activate the power of Air with its energy of inspiration, rushing winds that cut through inertia, harnessing the energies of vast skies in which there are no limits and imbuing that stone with those qualities.

But which stone do you use? What incense? The answers that make sense to you have to do with your correspondences. There are typical answers to those questions, and I'll be sharing whole lists of them in Chapter Two: Correspondences. But if, for example, you have a favorite stone that you picked up on an excellent trip that you took, that could easily be the one you use regardless of what this book or anyone else tells you. Perhaps we choose a specific deity to assist us in our journey: Poseidon for a sea journey or Janus if worried about having trouble crossing a border. In the same way that non-verbal cues can make up as much or more of a conversation with someone as the words you speak, the correspondences you use during your work help to communicate your message in more subtle and nuanced ways than the text of your spell on its own.

At this stage, the keyword is *creating*.

Powering Our Magic

This step connects energy to magic like a flashlight battery or plugging into an electrical socket. While the energy we use to power our magic can come entirely from within (the most likely case when working spontaneously), it is often more powerful when fueled by forces outside of ourselves. How you do this depends on your path. For example, if you have a relationship with a particular deity or aspect, this is where you would extoll them to take a hand in your magic. If your connection is with the element of Earth, then now is when you want to ensure you're making good contact with bare soil. You get the idea. However it is that you go about it in your practice, this is the step of the process to manifest your energy.

The method you use in the raising is independent of where you derive power. You might create a chant, the repetitive phrasing of which will focus and amplify power. Some members of my coven are drawn to dancing. They will gradually dance faster or drum with growing fervor while visualizing and feeling the energy raised increasing in size and intensity. Others prefer to sit silently and still, meditating while visualizing their growing power. Any of these methods could connect you and, for example, your patron deity, unless They have an aversion to or conflict with the activity (given Her frequent conflicts with Poseidon, I would not call upon Athena, for example, to watch over you as you cross the Aegean Sea).

As the power builds, I recommend creating what is known as a *cone of power*. This is entirely a process of conception (although if having a physical cone helps you focus, use one). Doing so brings the energy swirling around you into focus, making it far more easily directed. Think of water pressure in your shower or kitchen sink: tighter and more forceful spray is achieved by narrowing the aperture through which water flows, likewise with magical energy. Using this shape, like the pyramid, concentrates energy in a narrowing shape to reach a pinnacle of power, which can then be released at the end of the ritual to carry your intent into the cosmos. If a cone feels wrong, use a circle or any shape that works for you.

Whatever visualization you select, in some way, you'll want a shaping or channeling aspect to your power raising; otherwise, you're likely to have a diffused cloud of energy gathering about you. I don't know about you, but pointing in the distance and telling a cloud to "hop on it!" doesn't sound like the best choice. Joking aside, not using the cone or some other method doesn't make your magic fail, but it is another place where you can make things easier or harder on yourself, depending on your choices.

I am a visual thinker, as are many people, so my descriptive language tends to lean into terminology like "visualize" and "see." If you are better at sensing energy in ways other than visual, alter the language to fit your needs better. For example, if you feel energy (tactile), then your cone of power might be a shape you form. If you taste energy, you may wrap the energy in a kind of tortilla to direct it. Maybe you smell the energy's fragrance as it wafts from a scented candle you've used to power your spell into your nose, preparing for a final, deep release of air and energy through breath in the next stage. Perhaps you hear the rhythm of the energy, a steady beat building in power until it reaches a crescendo (and an accompanying drum to keep your timing). In every case, taking the diffused energy you've collected and preparing to point it toward a specific outcome is essential.

At this stage, the keyword is *growing*.

Releasing the Energy

Finally, when you can't add any more power and feel like you're going to burst from all that you've raised, release the energy to do its work. This energy might be pushed into a charm or talisman, into another person, or sent up and into the universe; wherever it goes is where you want it to do its work. It is vitally important to remember that this is not your cue to relax your focus. You will likely begin to feel a natural sag or drop as all that energy leaves you; this is normal and expected. However, moving energy is rarely an immediate process. You can begin to feel the effect of the energy leaving you well before the job is done, so be careful. Keep yourself locked on to your intentions just as much as before. Center your goal in your mind as you move everything that you've gathered towards your goal. You'll know when you're done. Honestly, when you've done this a few times, it's unlikely you'll be caught off-guard by the sensation of the energy leaving you.

After you send the energy off, make sure to ground yourself once again. I like to imagine the remnants of any energy I've gathered dripping down inside my legs and pooling in my feet before letting it leech harmlessly into the earth. Working with magic can be potent: it's vital that you ground if you are feeling "up" or more energetic than when you started. That isn't you, it's the energy you collected, and it will harm you if you don't get rid of it safely.

When directing energy, we often use a physical gesture to indicate where we want it to go. If I am alone, I like to fling my arms into the air, using a big throwing up-and-out movement—picture a "ta-da" gesture from a stage magician or someone releasing a dove into the air. However, a gesture that big isn't strictly necessary, so when I am in public, I use a quick flip of my right index finger. If your focus is on an object (a charm or a protection ward), you'll probably want to hold the object and channel the energy you've gathered through your arms and out of your hands.

If you intend to push energy into an object, you'll want to plan and consider how to keep it with you for the best effect. Obvious candidates are jewelry, such as a necklace or ring, or another personal item you would always keep with you, like a keychain. Remember, if you aren't "out" in your community or need to keep your actions discreet, your token isn't required to be "witchy." You could use a semi-precious stone that makes a suitable correspondence to your magical intent and set that on a necklace. I have a small wire cage, maybe an inch long, attached to my keychain. For an extended period, I kept a black tourmaline in it, which in my practice is aligned with transforming negative energy into positive. Now and then, the little stone in the cage would break, indicating to me that it had done as much as it could do, and I'd replace it. Anyone who saw it might think it was a little unusual, but not anything to arouse suspicion (while I haven't been in the "broom closet" since the early 2000s, I had a mundane office job for most of my life, and I purposefully avoided bringing attention to myself).

My husband is enamored with a set of *komboloi*, a Greek version of worry beads, that he often has on him (he calls them his adult fidget spinners). They look like rosary beads, and nobody has ever batted an eye as he swings them around his hand or moves the beads one by one along the string. Something like that can make an ideal choice for a talisman as part of a spell. It might be unusual, but, at most, it will only spark some (easily deflected) curiosity. Of course, go nuts if you're out and in a Pagan-friendly environment. Ram horns with silver bangles, necklaces with a Hekate talisman hanging from them—the (magical) world is your oyster.

At this stage, the keyword is *directing*.

Energy Work

The thesis statement for a school essay on energy work might go something like: "Witches perform magic by accessing and manipulating energy within a symbolic framework to produce a specific effect." We've talked about the broad strokes of our method, but the nuts and bolts still need to be examined to ensure that I will be speaking clearly to you as we go along.

You likely noticed that each of the four basic steps was based on working with energy, with physical implements acting in a supporting role. After all, at this thirty-thousand-foot view, all magic can be described the same way: decide, devise, draw, and direct.

Witches work with the energy around us that makes up the fabric of the physical plane. There are as many concepts of the nature of the energy we work with as traditions and there are practices doing the work. Some try to reconcile the natural and supernatural worlds, perhaps envisioning the atoms that make up all matter, with the spark of positive and negative attraction existing (almost) as far down as we can observe. Another amalgamative method is to lean into the advancements in quantum science, pointing to the fact that behaviors are being discovered which can be observed but not explained; magic could be from this realm, it is said.

Meanwhile, some forgo any attempt to explain magical energy scientifically; a popular model along these lines is that there is a connecting force between all living things. This connection explains all manner of observed metaphysical phenomena (twins experiencing each other's lives in small ways, for example). Still, it also implies that, as we are all connected, we can draw from this vast pool of shared vitality to power our magic. Of course, some believe in personified deities and acknowledge such figures as bestowers of power. Just as with my advice on your magical intention earlier, your concept of energy (whichever gives you a handhold of understanding) should be clear in your mind. After all, if you don't know what you expect to find when you reach out, the odds that you'll find what you're looking for are…well, poor.

An excellent place to start is with our personal energy, which emanates within and from ourselves. This energy includes our metabolism, heat, and the force some practices call *chi* or *ki*. This also has the benefit of not requiring any leveraging of external sources. The great thing about using ourselves as energy sources is that, while we are not inexhaustible, we are infinitely replenishing. Our energy can be affected by ordinary means: we recharge ourselves by eating, exercising, and sleeping. We also gather strength from friends and loved ones, as well as from hobbies and activities we enjoy, such as music. Naturally, inhibiting or draining our energy via illness, overwork, or self-neglect is possible. Your energy balance is also affected by emotions, psychological issues, and spiritual exertions. All these influences and energies are interrelated in complicated ways that can be beneficial (such as when we push ourselves to accomplish something, like staying up all night to meet an unexpected deadline) or harmful (such as "self-medicating" psychic wounds with drugs, food, or alcohol). It is straightforward advice to tell you, "Hey, take care of yourself; it's good for you." However, if you're new to this, you should be aware that you are creating a new drain on yourself, and the conditions you maintain for yourself are more important than ever.

Over the years, I've had plenty of students in my Art of Ritual class complaining of feeling tired or run-down a few months in. When we review what they're doing in class and then ask them what else has changed in their lives, they usually say, "Nothing, really." Bingo! Magic is terrific; you can achieve so much with it, but it's not free. You must make more frequent deposits in the "Bank of You" to prepare for these new withdrawals.

Sensing Energy

When we work with energy within ourselves or elsewhere, the first step is to change it from an amorphous concept. We've got to put our arms around it, feel it, and know it. If you're not new to energy work, this is probably an old hat for you. But a review never hurts, right?

To sense your energy, start by getting comfortable. I recommend sitting in a chair with your feet on the floor and your hands resting on your thighs. The chair should let you sit in a neutral position, not so high that your feet dangle and not so low that your knees bend uncomfortably. Breathe calmly and allow your head and body to release any negativity. Let any worries and mundane concerns fall away. Continue to breathe evenly throughout this exercise and the next. It is unnecessary to do "special breathing" of any sort, nothing that requires you to "manage" the process. Bring yourself, as much as you can, to a neutral state.

A simple technique for sensing energy is to rub your palms together for about ten seconds, creating friction (your palms will likely feel warm). Then, move your hands apart several inches and pay attention to any sensations emanating from your palms. Where do you begin to sense a change in how it feels? How does it change? If you don't feel anything at all, that's fine. This isn't a binary pass/fail thing. Try it several times, pausing for a minute or so between attempts. Bring yourself back to neutral before each attempt.

Once you recognize a shift in sensation, slowly move your palms together until you feel a sense of resistance or a shift in temperature. This might feel like warmth, heat, a decrease in temperature, or even downright cold. Instead of temperature, it might feel denser or lighter, or be a tingling sensation. People experience energy differently.

Manipulating Energy

As you read in the earlier sections, eventually, you will be doing all sorts of things with energy. But, if this is new for you, let's walk a little before we run. Only once you can sense the energy from the previous exercise can you start manipulating and playing with it.

For example, imagine the sensations from the previous exercise as light; this lets you start to visualize what might otherwise be wholly invisible forces. Imagine it clearly and powerfully. You should be able to describe it, even if only to yourself. Does it have color? A texture? A smell? A taste? A sound? What shape is it in? How big is it?

Once you have a firm idea of what you're sensing, let's take it a step further. Slowly pull your hands apart and shape that light into a ball hovering between your palms, not quite touching you. How big can you make the ball? How small? Does it change in intensity or warmth as you change the size? Is it still the same color? After a few moments, long enough to feel stable and in control in the new position, bring your hands together and allow the light to dissipate.

If this is your first time, or even early in your practice, don't be surprised that you don't just knock these down one after the other in a few minutes. Yes, some people have that affinity and instantly grasp what they're doing, but it is far more common for this to be a process. I've had students who felt they had to "fake it" in our classes because they didn't have the "aha!" moment as quickly as others, but it always came to them as they kept trying. After that moment, catching up is comparatively easy.

When learning to sense and manipulate energy, always ground any excess energy when finished. We just talked about this; my method is to visualize excess energy running down my legs and through the soles of my feet into the earth. You should feel calm, perhaps slightly energized or refreshed, but neither "up" nor "down." If anything feels off, work through your grounding exercise again.

MEDITATION

In any situation, your responses alter and affect the environment and how others react to you, even if it's not a clear and precise action/reaction effect. Generally speaking, if your response is highly emotional, the situation will become more intense; if it is calmer, it will often shift the feeling to a more neutral scenario. As Witches, we recognize that we are responsible for our reactions and the energy we bring into situations. So, the more neutral, reasoned, calm, and positive our energy output, the more that energy will exist in our environment.

To remain calm under stressful situations, I strongly recommend learning to meditate. I know you have plenty of things to do. But most of us end up overeating, playing too many games, drinking too much, and doing everything but being intentional and conscious. When we avoid being intentional, we become reactive, rather than proactive or neutral, losing control and focus.

Meditation does not need to be anything complicated. It's a matter of sitting comfortably and picking something to focus on: your breath, a candle, some soft repetitive music, or nature sounds. When you catch your mind wandering (which it will), don't berate yourself or consider the meditation session a failure. The best thing to do is observe yourself thinking extraneous thoughts. For example, you're sitting quietly, paying attention to your breathing. After a minute or two into it, you realize that you're actually thinking about your list of errands to run that day. Don't try and squash the thought, which ends up with you fighting with yourself over what you should be thinking (sounds exhausting just reading about it, right?); instead, "pull the camera back," so to speak, and notice yourself thinking about the errands. Chances are that this conscious focus on the thought will cause it to drain away, which is a better result than battling yourself with taciturn demands to "stop thinking."

If you're worried about doing this practice "right," let me stop you there. There is no right; there is only doing. The point of meditation is not to silence our thoughts, but to let them pass by. It has been said in many places by many people that if you are thinking about the "quality" of your meditation, then you are meditating. The conscious observation of what is going on in your head is the point of meditation. Accept at the outset that there will not be silence in your head through your whole meditation and know that the point is not about silence; it's about flow. Thoughts flow in; we observe them and allow them to flow out.

With practice, you'll find that you can observe your thoughts and exert more control than ever over them. At its core, meditation is a kind of relaxed concentration to direct toward anything you wish: simple actions (chores), eating (savoring every bite and drink), a goal (an affirmation), or nothing at all. Meditation can be incorporated into daily activities by paying attention. Keep track of where your feet or hands are always. Notice the flavor and texture of what you consume. Lose yourself in chores like washing dishes or sweeping.

Most people succeed at meditation when they follow a few core steps:

1. Create a quiet space where you won't be disturbed.
2. Set a timer for one minute to start. When you succeed at meditating for a minute, increase it to two minutes, then three, and so forth until you feel like you have good practice going.
3. Try to meditate at the same time every day.
4. Avoid meditating on a full stomach, when overly tired, or while wearing restrictive clothing.
5. Don't meditate while under the influence of alcohol or drugs. Some medications can interfere with our ability to be calm and focused. Use your best judgment.

Meditating while you travel is possible, I promise. You can meditate if you can find a place to sit, whether in a car, in a corner of the airport, or on a train. Here's how I make sure to have time and the mental space to meditate:

1. Add at least fifteen minutes on top of your most generous estimate of what you'll need to clear security and other travel

administrative tasks. This may only work for the first stage of travel, but it helps set the intention for the entire journey.[13]

2. Sit down, preferably somewhere a bit out of the way.
3. Take ten deep breaths over at least three minutes. (To breathe consciously, see the next section).
4. Set a timer and follow your breath for whatever period you choose. Inhale through your nose for a count of four, hold your breath for a count of four, release your breath over a count of four, then pause for a count of four. Repeat until the timer sounds.

I like to travel with a tiny MP3 player (what can I say? The Walkman was a huge step forward in music for me). I have a specific track I play for meditation so I don't need to set a timer; I find an out-of-the-way place, pop in the earbuds, and shift my consciousness into a new place.

I sat on a stone that had been placed exactly here thousands of years ago. We were at the Beaghmore Stone Circles in Northern Ireland, and I felt a powerful connection to the land. "I'm going to meditate for a bit," I told my husband. He grinned and wandered toward a different part so as not to distract me, long used to my taking time for meditation when I felt called to do so. As I breathed, I felt the connection grow stronger as the land recognized me. My ancestors had been here worshiping the natural cycles, following the sun's path through the seasons. After my brief respite, I opened my eyes, only to discover that it had been more like thirty minutes. My bottom was very cold, and I had difficulty standing up. Worth it, but ouch!

13 The fifteen minutes is just for you to have time to meditate, not a suggestion for arrival time!

Breathwork

When we are stressed, our breathing changes, becoming faster and originating from higher in the chest than when we are calm and relaxed. When we deliberately breathe deeper and slower, we stimulate the vagus nerve, which activates the so-called "flight or fight" reflex.[14]

Creating a breathwork practice allows us to be consciously aware and sense/feel/hear through our bodies. When we stop breathing easily, our bodies tense, our senses dull, and our mind gets frantic. In a sense, we lose consciousness, feeling apart and sensing something lacking.

When you first begin to breathe consciously, wear loose clothing and make sure your nostrils are clear. If you have a cold, allergies, or even a sore throat, wait until it's cleared before you begin; you must use your nose and a clear throat in this exercise. More than anything, don't get discouraged.

Here is a technique for learning to breathe consciously:

1. Place one hand on your abdomen right beneath your ribcage.
2. Take a slow, deep breath; feel your stomach rise as the breath moves down to your lungs.
3. Pause for a moment.
4. Slowly release the breath, sighing quietly and allowing your shoulders to drop as you fully exhale.
5. Pause briefly and repeat until you have completed ten slow, full abdominal breaths. Try to keep your breathing smooth and regular without gulping in a big breath or letting your breath out all at once.

Over the years, I've done this exercise so often that the simple act of placing my hand on that place on my body will shift my breathing into a more relaxed pattern. I created a trigger with that physical gesture, one subtle enough that it can be done almost anywhere.

---

14 There is a ton of recent research on this nerve and how intertwined it is with the mind-body connection. I recommend Edith Zimmerman's article "I Now Suspect the Vagus Nerve Is the Key to Well-being," *The Cut* (9 May 2019) www.thecut.com/2019/05/i-now-suspect-the-vagus-nerve-is-the-key-to-well-being.html.

As Above, So Below

A phrase you might hear Witches say from time to time, "As Above, So Below," refers to the idea that we individuals are microcosms of the larger universe. What we can conceive of can manifest through applying our will to specific energetic forces. We are gods in the making, growing in our abilities and knowledge, becoming better people, thereby making the world around us better.

The word "macrocosm" comes from the Greek *makros kosmos*, "the great world," meaning the universe in its entirety. Microcosm comes from the Greek *mikros kosmos*, "the small world," and refers to a human being understood as a miniature universe. Again, the concept is that natural processes in our existence echo the world at large (and vice versa). One side effect of this notion is that our spiritual changes can create higher levels of consciousness that can be shared.

Sympathetic Magic

Once we grasp this microcosm/macrocosm connection, we want to apply it in our practice. Sympathetic magic is sometimes called "imitative magic" and refers to connecting a larger event or reality to a smaller personal item so that manipulating the item you have affects the larger one. This is the principle of *like produces like* (which some call the Law of Similarity)—that things that once were in contact *retain their connection* even after physical contact no longer exists (which some call the Law of Contact or Contagion). As I said earlier, some people see advancements in quantum science as a validation of this magic. I will leave that as an exercise for the reader.

Sympathetic magic involves creating a ritual that imitates what you desire to accomplish on the material plane on the inner or astral plane. Here, a spell for increasing money might have us growing a pot of basil seedlings (basil is an herb of prosperity). As you nurture the plant, you are nurturing your financial fortunes. This necessitates that you reset your focus any time you work with the plant; if you lose focus and start treating it as "just another" plant, you are signaling to the universe that you weren't serious about this spell.

Another example would be increasing one's fertility by making love at the edge of a newly ripening field, which is thought to be a practice going back to rural communities before Gerald Gardner's great-grandparents were born. Again, the microcosm/macrocosm works in both directions here. The couple seeking fertility is "working" in sympathy with the growing field. If they made a good connection, then their expenditure of procreative energy would billow out into the crops, helping them along for the coming season.

The Law of Similarity is the magic of believing walnuts are good for brain magic because the nuts look like the halves of a brain or that red beet juice is good for the blood— "like produces or equals like."

Two things to keep in mind for now: first, it's good to know that this is what led many folks to develop herbal lore (and similar) in the first place; they wouldn't keep giving people their special herbal tea if it didn't work, but they tried it in the first place because they believed that the similarities meant something. Second, as you are working on your personal language of symbols and correspondences, this is your free pass to discard lore that doesn't make sense to you. If you don't think walnuts look like a brain, you aren't going to believe yourself when you're doing magic with them, so don't use them. I can tell you this is a thing until I'm blue in the face, but if it isn't doing it for you, that is perfectly valid.

Although, in the current climate of "do whatever you want, there are no rules," I should note that I don't recommend you discard existing lore on a whim. A *lot* of people have done *a lot* of work over *a long* period of time working correspondences out. Giving the lore a try is, in most cases, probably going to save you a lot of time and effort.

The Law of Contagion is the belief that relationships can exist across time and space despite no physical connection, as seen in plenty of cultures. My husband gets a kick out of muttering, "They're wizards!" whenever we visit a European Catholic church with reliquaries of bits of saints, famous clothing, or similar. These tokens are often lavishly adorned, and parishioners pray at these objects, believing that these bodies of saints protect them. Certain traditions have practices centered on creating a doll that looks like another person and might contain that person's hair or nail clippings. As you might imagine, the idea is that you can use the doll to manipulate that person.

If I had to sum this chapter up in one sentence, it would be this: you don't need to believe in magic to use the methods and techniques throughout this book.

Chapter Two

Correspondences

Much of our work with symbols involves correspondences, and it's a big enough topic that it merits an entire chapter.

Correspondences are one of the things that make magic a practice rather than just something that lives in your head. This is where we get "crafty" and apply the theoretical to the practical. This chapter is very different from those in my previous books, as it focuses on using the symbology of correspondences to create spells and charms. While I will offer lots of tables and lists of items you can use with your travel magic, I also want you to understand why correspondences are used and how you can make deep connections.

These connections are everywhere. Once you begin to look at the world through a Witch's eyes, you will see that nothing exists in isolation; everything connects with something else. My spiritual life has long been a part of my mundane life in quiet, non-obvious ways.

Symbols Are Key

The word "symbol" comes from the Greek *symbolon*, meaning "token" or "sign." A symbol is something that stands for another object and takes the form of words, sounds, gestures, ideas, or visual images. For example, a red octagon often represents "stop," and a lion signifies strength. In magic, symbols are a language that can key you into concepts, ideas, and beliefs created over millennia of human history.

After a particularly awful plane landing in a thunderstorm, I found myself in the strange position of suddenly being afraid to fly. My head knew why I felt that way, but my younger self wasn't getting on a plane again. Instead of ignoring my fear, I sat with it for a few hours and asked what might relieve it. Finally, with some mental hiccupping from tears, Younger Self told me that if I sang to Mercury during take-off and landing, He would watch over us and see us home safely.

Doing my best, I crafted a (ridiculous) song and boarded the plane. It was hard; I was shaking and clammy with fear as I buckled in. Paying close attention to the safety instructions and taking deep, calming breaths helped ("See," I showed Younger Self, "they know what to do if anything goes wrong. Which it won't!"). Then, as we pulled away and along the tarmac, I took a deep breath and sang to Mercury.

"Winged Mercury, please come to me
Whether I cross the land or open sea
I ask you to protect me
Keep me
Safe from harm while I roam
Until my journeys safely take
Me home."

Not the world's best poetry, but that didn't matter. While I sang, I visualized Mercury as He stood on my altar, then stepping forward and enfolding me. I knew it worked when my heart stopped racing and I grew calm. Younger Self pronounced itself satisfied and left me alone the rest of the flight, although I sang my song again as we came in for a landing, just in case. Then I ended it with a "Thank you for your care, blessed be."

My song was silent, although deeply felt, and I still sing it when I fly.

Symbols Are Key

A symbol links concepts together. When you think of any canine, that concept and image are linked with the symbol "dog"; when you open that mental file, you access all the associations, good or bad, that you have about dogs. Of course, each image and concept connect to other concepts ("big dog," "mastiff," "hunting dog," and so on). Some symbols are unique to you and your lexicon, created from your life experiences. Someone bitten by a dog might associate "dog" with pain and fear; another might associate it as a symbol of companionship.

Symbols exist everywhere and are foundational to practicing magic. When you draw a dollar sign on a piece of green paper, you connect the symbol "$" with less concrete concepts of prosperity to bring more money into your life.

Symbols can be used in many ways in magic. Some examples include:

- **Drawn:** On physical objects, like paper or wood, using ink, pencil, charcoal, etc.
- **Crafted:** Out of clay, yarn, metal, or whatever you are interested in creating.
- **Printed:** Use your printer to create symbols from images others have created.

The only rule is to ensure that the symbol chosen is aligned with your intent and then included as an integral part of your magic.

Correspondences come from many places, but typically you will draw them from:

- **Tradition:** Most magical traditions have a specific set of symbols and language they work with. Wiccans, for example, align the element of Air with the direction East, the color red with energy, and silver with the goddess. Druids, Ceremonial Magicians, and other traditions have their systems.
- **Culture:** February 14 is a day to celebrate romance in many places. In Chinese culture, the color red symbolizes good luck.

Italians start their winter holiday on December 8 with the Feast of the Immaculate Conception and don't eat meat at their feast on Christmas Eve. In Iceland, they celebrate Jolabokaflod, during which they give one another books and then read until midnight while eating yummy food and drinking cocoa.

- **Family:** From nicknames to shorthand closings on messages, many families have a private language that is often mysterious to outsiders. My family often closes our emails with LY and our initial rather than anything more formal.
- **Personal:** My husband and I joke about how when we do (or say) something peculiar to our personalities, it's proof that aliens didn't abduct us. Some people have lucky socks or a shirt, and others have an image of a particular place, which evokes a good feeling within them when they see it. These are personal correspondences based entirely on our connections through our lived experiences.

Aligning Outer with Inner

Correspondences assist us in focusing our intent and directing our energy; they make overly large theoretical and philosophical notions more accessible and relatable. They link us to the past, tapping into our sense of place, family, and culture. They are like keys that unlock the connection between the physical/seen and the energetic/unseen.

When you work with correspondences, you'll start to see patterns and linkages, and I encourage you to keep track of these patterns when you come across them. A note file in your mobile phone or a notebook that you keep at hand—anything, so long as it is easily accessible because you can stumble upon these connections in your life at any time. For me, pine smells evoke memories of holiday celebrations, special food not made at any other time of year, and family events.

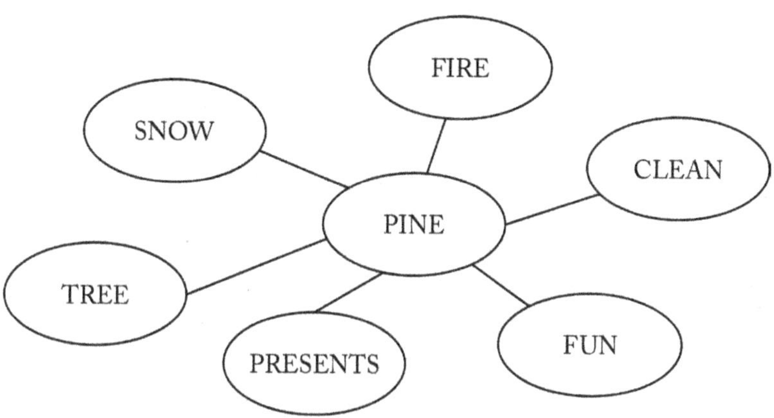

Pine Correspondences

Now, with just a little extra research and contemplation, your brain will start making other associations that link the primary connections from the concept of pine.

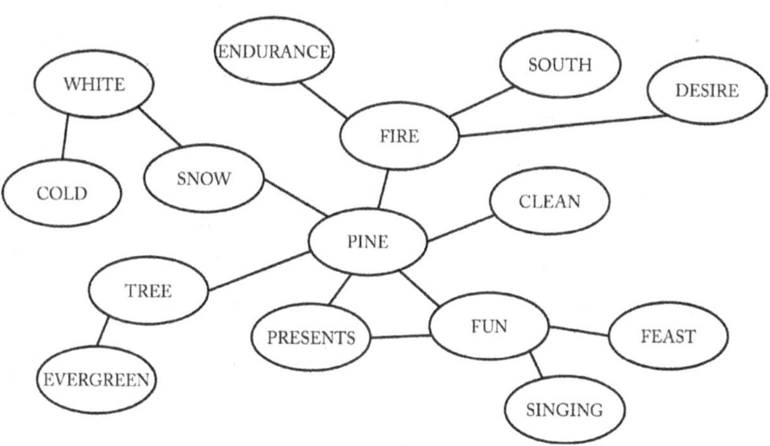

Further Pine Correspondence

Interrelationships

Our brains like to organize information by association, forming complex patterns. These patterns form on many levels: emotional, mental, social, and spiritual. When we receive new information, our brains link it to existing patterns, expanding the web of associations. These links and associations are utterly unique; how I create associations between symbols differs from how you will. This is why looking up equivalencies or using a spell someone else wrote is only the beginning of your work.

Modern psychology shows us how our brains are built to constantly make associations between the various aspects of our experience. Most of us can quickly (almost automatically) distinguish a dog's bark between warning, pain, and loneliness because knowing the difference in those sounds tells us whether to run away from, run to, or ignore the strange dog.

You may read a correspondence article online (or even in this book) and feel a fundamental disconnect. I can easily imagine the reader living in an area of scrub trees saying, "How could pine represent snow? That makes no sense to me at all!" When this inevitably happens to you, honor it. If you're trying to call up the sensations of winter for a spell as you prepare for a skiing trip, don't use pine incense because I told you to. If you disagree, it will not help, and you will likely be distracted because of this background dissonance. All anyone can do for you is suggest possible connections or connections that work for them.

When we use many symbols in our ritual, we reinforce the message. For a ski trip, you might use pine incense, an image of a skier flying down a pristine snow-covered hill, and crystals scattered like ice across a white altar cloth. The more you have, the more ways you'll be focusing on the goal of your magic.

When we take the time to realize and embrace our specific symbolic language, we create a clear vision of what we want to accomplish with our magic. Books, however, require us to impart information linearly. To combat that, I encourage you to think of every table as a starting point rather than an answer; and to try creating your webs of linkages with every spell or ritual you create.

A Collection of Correspondences

In collecting the data in this chapter, I focused on components aligned with and supportive of typical aspects of travel: abundance, adventure, Air, clarity, communication, Earth, Fire, happiness, healing, journey, luck, protection, relaxation, safety, success, travel, and Water. You will likely have personal keywords and items to add to this collection.

Many items have multiple connections, some of which may feel counter-intuitive. For example, cedar is an herb associated with Earth, but also summer. Remember to use what makes sense to you, what connects to your thoughts and feelings; don't just take my word for it!

Animals

Animals offer us an alliance with the natural world that can assist us in moving through their world. My process of assigning a connection to an animal involves looking at its natural habitat, cultural aspects, and any relevant mythology.

- **Aardvark:** Also called antbear, this "earth pig" is a solitary creature that prefers burrowing. A significant part of many African myths and folktales, Aardvark is helpful to call upon for assistance with solo journeys, especially those that focus on personal transformation.
- **Albatross:** There is a legend that Albatross never has to land, traveling the world by riding air currents everywhere. Its magic is that of freedom, hope, strength, wanderlust, and navigation.
- **Bat:** Depending on culture, the bat is a polarizing creature, seen as good fortune or the harbinger of death and misfortune. Various cultures see it as a warning of chaos, rebirth, unrealized potential, and prosperity. This is an animal to be clear about your feelings before working with; people either value or loathe the bat. Its ability to navigate dark and uncertain territory makes it a powerful ally.
- **Bear:** As part of their life cycle, bears often travel long distances, and their strength and connection to the land make them valuable

allies for travel. Work with them to increase your ability to roam freely and follow the path you desire (rather than one imposed upon you by others).

- **Butterfly:** Often seen as a sign of personal transformation, that energy is easily harnessed to use in travel magic. Butterflies only live a short time, but their life cycle offers energy towards becoming a new, better person. The monarch butterfly has intense travel energy as they migrate as much as three thousand miles yearly. Their colors echo health and wellness. My husband once found himself amid a migratory butterfly pattern entirely by chance; one moment, he was living normally. Then, he was suddenly within a tide of the fluttering insects for nearly an hour. It's an image he never has any problem calling up, and he loves using it for transitional purposes.
- **Camel:** Like all pack animals, camels symbolize travel and journeys. It also represents wisdom, endurance, survival, service, self-sufficiency, conservation, and stamina. With its life-storing humps filled with fat and water, Camel offers wisdom about pacing oneself and enduring hardship.
- **Chipmunk:** Surviving solely by luck guiding them to gather enough stores to make it through winter, call on Chipmunk when you need a hefty dose of luck to get you out of a challenging situation. If you do, follow the guidance given, no matter how unusual.
- **Crane:** Associated with the Sun and Water, the Crane is valuable for its ability to hide what is vulnerable, offering the traveler protection and secrecy while assisting with focusing on what's important.
- **Dolphin:** Fisherpeople have always viewed dolphins as good luck and bringers of safety. Their joyful attitude and curiosity make them good companions for adventurous journeys on the water.
- **Dragonfly:** This dazzling aerial acrobat is known for its fast flight, offering assistance with sudden direction changes. It is helpful for water and air travel, inhabiting both during its life.

- **Goose:** A bringer of luck when traveling to faraway, even legendary, places, Goose aids with communication, returning to one's home (migratory patterns), gaining a complete picture of what is ahead, and facilitating all journeys. It aids in all magic related to new travels to distant places.
- **Horse:** Associated with travel and freedom in many cultures, the long-ago domestication of Horse allowed people to explore far beyond their communities. Their assistance in any magic involving movement and travel is always helpful.
- **Hummingbird:** Fantastic, amazing flyers, hummingbirds are full of energy with wings that can flutter at over two hundred beats per second. In comparison, the human heart only beats between sixty and one hundred times per minute. This means that hummingbirds move their wings two hundred times more than the human heartbeat. Work with Hummingbird for all air travel, but mainly when it might be tricky, require special maneuvering, or high-speed travel. A reminder to take joy whenever possible, they can assist with rain magic, maximizing the enjoyment of a journey and accomplishing the seemingly impossible.
- **Ostrich:** Despite being the largest bird, Ostrich does not fly, making it a paradox. Work with ostrich when you need to get down to basics and make practical decisions in the face of ethereal, whimsical dreams. This is a fast-moving bird, offering assistance when you've got to get going, now!
- **(Sea) Gull:** All shallow water travel is protected by Gull, as is all air travel. Gull offers wisdom in communicating across cultures, diplomacy, and courtesy.
- **Wren:** One of the most resourceful and adaptable birds, Wren also offers general protection, but specifically against drowning. Offering a boost of energy, Wren suggests additional resources during your journey.

COLORS

All colors can be useful, depending on your perspective, needs, and personal choice. Remember that white is the universal color, but if all you have are colored birthday candles, use what's available.

- **Black:** Absorbs negativity in all forms. Offers protection.
- **Blue:** Healing. Enhances psychic abilities; promotes peace, wisdom, and understanding.
- **Brown:** Material increase and financial success; issues regarding housing and friendship. Supports decision-making when offered too many alternatives. Improves concentration. Use when working with animals and finding lost objects.
- **Gray:** Useful when pondering complex issues. Negates or neutralizes a negative influence. Offers neutrality and can break a stalemate.
- **Green:** Finances and money; employment. Fertility and growth. Prosperity, luck, and success.
- **Orange:** Stimulates encouragement, adaptability, stimulation, and attraction. Business and career goals, property deals, ambition, general success, justice, legal matters, selling, action.
- **Pink:** Supports honor, love, friendship, morality, healing of emotions, peace, caring, and nurturing.
- **Purple:** Eases tension, promotes ambition, business, progress, success, power, healing of disease, spirituality, and psychic manifestations. Reveals hidden knowledge. Promotes travel, writing, learning, higher education, and wisdom.
- **Red:** Ideal for protection, career struggles, issues requiring fast action, survival, strength, courage, health, vigor, sexual love, and passion. Increases magnetism in rituals.
- **White:** A balance of all colors. Spiritual enlightenment, cleansing, clairvoyance, healing, truth-seeking, purity, purification, sincerity, protection, peace. It can substitute for any other color.
- **Yellow:** Stimulates intelligence, supports divination and creativity, attraction, persuasion, charm, and confidence. It breaks mental blocks.

METALS

- **Aluminum:** A modern metal, there is no ancient history of use to draw upon. However, given the ubiquitous presence of aluminum in so many forms of travel—airplanes, boats, cars, etc.—it makes sense to consider using it in travel magic. You might wrap a stone or image in aluminum foil or fold the foil into the shape of the vehicle you will travel in.
- **Copper:** Use in spells for passion, money goals, professional growth, fertility, and business or career maneuvers.
- **Gold:** Promotes winning and happiness. Fosters understanding. Beneficial in rituals to bring about fast luck or money.
- **Silver:** Best in magic involving dreams or astral energies. Removes negativity and encourages stability, helps develop psychic abilities.

ELEMENTS

The four elements make up all matter and are one of the most accessible types of energy to align with to power our spells. Adding a bit of relevant elemental energy will do nicely if no other correspondences are possible for you.

For travel specifically:

- **Air:** All travel (but especially by plane).
- **Fire:** Not much used, but perhaps steam-based travel.
- **Water:** All water travel.
- **Earth:** All land-based travel, such as trains and cars.

Element of Earth

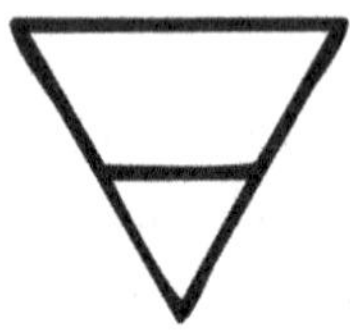

Earth is the element most of us understand the best. It represents not only the physical ground, but also the qualities of stability, reality, the material world, fertility, physical health, protection, wealth, home, and all land-based travel, such as trains and cars. It is upon Earth that the other three elements rest.

Compass point	North
Season	Winter
Time of Day	Midnight
Colors	All shades of green, brown, and black
Stones	All rocks and stones, but especially Rock Crystal, Malachite, Moss Agate, and Jade
Incense	Storax, Dittany of Crete, Benzoin
Zodiac signs and rulers	Capricorn, Taurus, and Virgo; Venus, Saturn
Herbs	Pine, grains, nuts, comfrey, oak, ivy, oats, rice, rye, wheat, vetiver, mosses, lichens, nuts, aloeswood, amber, makko (tabu noki), mugwort, patchouli, red cedar, vetiver, wild lettuce, yohimbe
Animals	All land animals, wolves, mice, and underground dwellers (moles, meerkats, etc.)

Element of Water

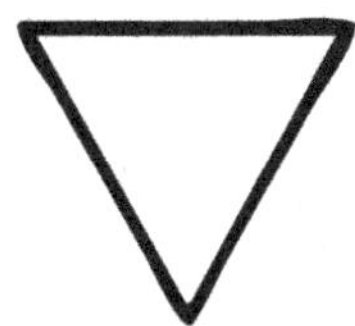

Water energy is the easiest to work with, whether from a puddle or faucet. The energy is similar to Air, but not as physically destructive as Earth or Fire. This energy is most potent during a storm, but is more valuable for reflection and the stimulation of psychic powers. Water energy can be drawn and used for dreaming, prophecy, divination, emotion, intuition, psychic abilities, empathy, emotional health, birth, mystery, moon magic, dreams, and spiritual cleansing.

Compass point	West
Season	Autumn
Time of Day	Sunset
Colors	All shades of blue
Stones	Aquamarine, opal, pearl
Incense	Myrrh
Zodiac signs and rulers	Cancer, Scorpio, and Pisces; Moon, Venus
Herbs	Seaweed, calamus, camphor, cardamom, catnip, chamomile, coltsfoot, costus, eucalyptus, hibiscus, Irish moss, myrrh, myrtle, sandalwood (yellow), spikenard, thyme, tonka bean, tragacanth gum, valerian, white willow
Animals	All water creatures, dolphins, fish, and whales

Element of Fire

Fire energy is the devouring power of intense emotions: anger, lust, and love. Like the element itself, it isn't easy to control and can potentially destroy everything it touches. When contained, Fire energy reveals truth as well as fueling spells. It is most potent when out of control (burning buildings or forest fires), but practically useless. Fire rules passion, action, sex, confidence, desire, strength, inspiration, and courage. A contained flame in a candle or hot coals is more valuable; enough for magic, but not enough to overpower us.

Compass point	South
Season	Summer
Time of Day	Midday
Colors	All shades of red, orange
Stones	Carnelian, tiger's eye, ruby, garnet, jet
Incense	Frankincense
Zodiac signs and rulers	Aries, Leo, and Sagittarius; Sun, Mars, Jupiter
Herbs	Allspice, bay leaf (laurel), cedar, cinnamon, clove, copal, damiana, dragon's blood, frankincense, galangal, ginger, golden seal, guar gum, hyssop, juniper, pennyroyal, rosemary, saffron, tarragon, turmeric, woodruff
Animals	Salamanders, dragons, snakes, and lizards

Element of Air

Air energy is more subtle than the other elements. It is in the air we breathe as much as the wind blowing over the hills. Air energy is light and can feel like any temperature when you work with it. It is most potent during a storm when lightning charges the air and the wind blows fast. Air energy does not have as much physical power as Earth or Fire energy, but it has significant advantages. It is the energy of intelligence, thoughts, overcoming blockages, new beginnings, memory, learning intellect, wisdom, understanding, communication, and friendship.

Compass point	East
Season	Spring
Time of Day	Dawn
Colors	Yellow and pastels
Stones	Clear quartz, citrine
Incense	Sandalwood
Zodiac signs and rulers	Gemini, Libra, and Aquarius; Jupiter, Mercury
Herbs	Acacia, anise, benzoin, gum arabic, horehound, hops, lavender, lemongrass, marjoram, mastic, oakmoss, palo santo, parsley, pine, sage, sandalwood (red), star anise
Animals	All winged creatures, birds, butterflies

PLANT ALLIES

This section includes using plants not just as herbs, but in the form of trees, essential oils, and incense. You can find many of them in grocery stores, although some will require a visit to an herbalist. Although there are many (many!) herbs and trees that can be an ally to the traveler, I confined my list to those that are most easily found. Aloeswood, for example, is often listed as an ally when doing magical cleansing, but it's an item you often have to special order. If I know of a specific preparation or use, I have mentioned it (such as benzoin, which is only used as incense).

Caution: All information is offered in good faith and should be understood as a general reference. No part of this information should be construed as medical advice. Using herbs in any form can have unintended—even dangerous—side effects. *Always* check the toxicity levels of plants you work with, even in small amounts. If you are pregnant or work with children, be especially careful.

SPECIFIC PURPOSES

- **Abundance:** Allspice, flour/grains, grapes, lemon, oakmoss, oil, olive(s), peppermint
- **Cleansing:** Anise, bay leaf (laurel), benzoin, chamomile, frankincense, parsley, rosemary, sandalwood, vetiver
- **Divination:** Cinnamon, comfrey, hops, mugwort, rosemary, sandalwood
- **Healing/Health:** Apple, ash, bay leaf (laurel), cedar, chamomile, cinnamon, elder, eucalyptus, horehound, juniper, lavender, marjoram, mugwort, myrrh, pine, rosemary, rowan, sandalwood, thyme
- **Luck:** Chamomile, cherry, cinnamon, clover, irish moss, dragon's blood, ginger, star anise
- **Money/Prosperity:** Ginger, irish moss, oakmoss, oak tree, prosperity
- **Protection:** Anise, ash, bay leaf (laurel), benzoin, cedar, cinnamon, clove, cypress, dragon's blood, eucalyptus, frankincense, hyssop, juniper, lavender, marjoram, mugwort, myrrh, oak, olive, oregano, parsley, pine, rosemary, sandalwood
- **Sleep:** Chamomile, hops, lavender, rosemary, thyme, valerian

- **Strength:** Cedar, cinnamon, dragon's blood, ginger, mugwort, saffron, tarragon
- **Success:** Basil, bayberry, cinnamon, clove, clover, ginger
- **Travel:** Ash, mugwort

Specific Plants

I travel with herbs wrapped in small squares of parchment paper (sometimes called baking paper). The waxy coating helps keep the herbs fresh, even when I'm out for weeks.

- **Allspice (*Pimenta dioica*):** Named for its aroma that seems made up of cinnamon, cloves, nutmeg, and pepper, this is an excellent ally when working all kinds of abundance, money, and prosperity magic (it can replace any of the plants it smells like!). The whole dried "peppercorns" are easily added to a charm bag.
- **Anise (Aniseed, *Pimpinella anisum*):** Aids sleep by warding off nightmares; helps find contentment and happiness when used in a charm bag (Note: Anise and Star Anise are not the same, but have a similar smell).
- **Apple (*Malus domestica*):** Excellent for money spells, longevity, and bringing the knowledge you need to you. An easy apple spell is to carve your need into the skin, then bury the fruit or throw it into a river or other body of moving water.
- **Ash (*Fraxinus excelsior*):** In Norse traditions, the world tree Yggdrasil is an ash tree. This association makes it an excellent wood for facilitating travel, especially between the worlds. This versatile tree is used for prosperity, health, and protection.
- **Basil (*Ocimum basilicum*):** Associated with money magic (tuck a pinch into your wallet to attract or keep money there). Sprinkle around the ritual area to cleanse it of unwanted energy.
- **Bay Leaf (*Laurus nobilis*):** Dried, the leaves make excellent petition paper. Tuck the leaves into a charm bag to invite protection, ward off evil, and turn away envy or jealousy.
- **Benzoin (*Styrax benzoin*):** Used as incense when combined with other ingredients (alone, it is overwhelming). Sacred to Mercury and, therefore, valuable for travel spells.

- **Cedar (*Cedrus*):** Used in magic to attract wealth, purification, cleansing, and protection.
- **Chamomile (*Matricaria chamomilla*):** Strongly associated with the Sun, use this to bring peace and calm in uncertain situations. Attracts good fortune, especially in all areas involving money.
- **Cherry (*Prunus avium*):** Particularly revered in Japan for its power to attract good fortune, new beginnings, and renewal. Its flowers and fruit are a food source for many, so it has powerful magic when used in magic for abundance.
- **Cinnamon (*Cinnamomum verum*):** Used to give an extra boost to any magic. It can replace an athame when cleansing or consecrating a space for ritual use. Assists in connecting with inner resources when needed. Use in any prosperity or divination work.
- **Clove (*Syzygium aromaticum*):** Add the whole dried flowers to a charm bag to protect, ward off jealousy, and bring prosperity.
- **Clover (*Trifolium*):** Money and protection magic. An old charm is to put a bit of clover in your left shoe to free you from negativity on the road.
- **Coffee (*Coffea*):** I never particularly liked the coffee I drank in the United States; it often tasted somewhat burnt and required lots of cream and sugar to make it palatable. Despite that, I always used coffee for abundance magic to speed things up and get them moving. Use a stick of cinnamon to stir your coffee as an easy way to manifest health, protection, strength, and success.
- **Comfrey (*Symphytum*):** Offers outstanding protective magic. When used in divination magic, it enhances intuition. Used to keep travelers safe and alert by keeping them grounded. Strengthens energy shields and protects the home, luggage, or automobile from theft. Use for protection and an easy journey in your travel spells.
- **Dragon's Blood (*Croton lechleri*):** Made from the sap of many different trees, it is traditionally used to make ink with which to write petitions or anoint candles in magic concerning courage, luck, and protection.

- **Eucalyptus (*Eucalyptus globulus*):** Just smelling fresh leaves or essential oil clears the mind and promotes healing. Although some sources say it makes a nice incense, I do *not* recommend burning it; the oil in the leaves can irritate the eyes and lungs.
- **Flour/Grains:** Because of their ability to create food, both for offering and to sustain life, all grains are symbolic of abundance. If you have enough extra grain to sacrifice as an offering, you're doing okay (and when you don't, it only strengthens the sacrifice).
- **Frankincense (*Boswellia sacra*):** Used as incense to purify the ritual space, lift the spirits, and boost any protective working.
- **Ginger (*Zingiber officinale*):** Combine with a silver coin and oak leaf to create a charm bag for luck and prosperity.
- **Grapes (*Vitis vinifera*):** With connections to many religions, grapes (and wine) are associated with abundance and good luck. Often enjoyed by royalty and the wealthy, their color can orient their energy: green for wealth, red for energy, and purple for spiritual matters.
- **Hops (*Humulus lupulus*):** Often used in magical pillows to promote dream workings. Cleanses and removes obstacles; focuses and calms the mind.
- **Hyssop (*Hyssopus officinalis*):** Offers potent protection against negative energies. Used to cleanse ritual space when made into a weak tea.
- **Irish Moss (Carrageen, *Chondrus crispus*):** A form of seaweed—therefore tied to all magic involving sea travel. Also valuable for money magic.
- **Juniper (*Juniperus communis*):** Used to attract wealth, purification, and cleansing. Strongly protective and dispels any negative energy.
- **Lavender (*Lavandula*):** Excellent when used for protection and healing. Sacred to Mercury.
- **Lemon (fruit and tree; *Citrus limon*):** Associated with joy, purification, and healing.

- **Marjoram (*Origanum majorana*):** Used in all workings involving bringing luck and joy.
- **Mint (*Mentha piperita i.* [peppermint] and *Mentha spicata L.* [spearmint]):** Promotes healing, the ability to gain money, and successful travel. Clears the mind and helps focus your intent.
- **Mugwort (*Artemisia vulgaris*):** Used for protection during travel; the scent is refreshing.
- **Myrrh (*Commiphora myrrha*):** Used as incense to purify the ritual space, lift the spirits, and invite a boost to any protective working.
- **Oakmoss (*Evernia prunastri*):** A kind of lichen (it was easily found when I lived in the Pacific Northwest), it is superb for grounding and connecting with the energy of forest areas. Excellent for money magic and abundance.
- **Oak (tree, *Quercus*):** Associated with Jupiter and Hecate, this can be a valuable ally in travel magic, particularly when making decisions, asking for guidance, and looking to increase prosperity.
- **Oil:** All oils symbolize abundance because of their ability to create food, both for offering and sustaining life. My (Polish) grandmother taught me that gifting a new household with salt, oil, and fresh bread ensures they never go hungry or want anything. In particular, olive oil has been considered sacred since ancient history.
- **Olive (fruit, oil, and tree; *Olea europaea*):** With its roots as much as 37,000 years old, the olive has an ancient reputation as a symbol of abundance, peace, and prosperity.
- **Oregano (*Origanum vulgare*):** Good substitute for St. John's Wort (*Hypericum perforatum*) in traditional spells for protection.
- **Parsley (*Petroselinum crispum*):** Used in workings calling for courage and enduring through adversity. May offer direction through tricky circumstances.
- **Pepper, Black (*Piper nigrum*):** Useful in any magical work for an extra power boost or when it involves money. Promotes strength and courage.

- **Pine (*Pinus*):** When bound together with a bit of thread, the needles make an excellent aspergillum for ritual-infused waters. Because its needles remain green throughout the year, it's associated with longevity. It also offers protection and prosperity.
- **Rosemary (*Salvia rosmarinus*):** Outstandingly protective, this is one of the best-known magical plants. It cleanses and creates sacred space by burning or using it to sprinkle clean water or other ritual-infused liquids. Offers strength, mental clarity, increased intuition, and access to dream messages.
- **Sandalwood (*Santalum album*):** My favorite incense. Balances one's emotions and mental state when surrounded by upheaval. Stress reliever. Enhances contact with the divine, making it valuable for any divination.
- **Star Anise (*Illicium verum*):** As an essential oil, star anise is useful in cleansing magic as well as protecting against negative energies and attracting good energy. Burn as incense as an offering to one's deity (Note: anise and star anise are not the same, but have a similar smell).
- **Thyme (*Thymus vulgaris*):** Useful addition to all magic relating to protection and cleansing.
- **Turmeric (*Curcuma longa*):** Effective in all travel related to business or work. Useful in work relating to getting healthy.
- **Vetiver (*Chrysopogon zizanioides*):** Used as an essential oil for magic involving grounding, increased concentration, awareness, manifestation, and prosperity. Assists in relaxation.
- **Willow (*Salix*):** A powerful force for self-rejuvenation and healing, this is the ally to reach for in any magic involving the enhancement or return of vitality. Associated with fresh water.
- **Wormwood (*Artemisia absinthium*):** Protects against bewitchment and unhealthy influence from another. It secures vehicles from accidents and keeps your travel safe.

Planetary Influencers

While not particularly useful while traveling, being able to time your spellwork and divination to the planets' energy can be a massive boost to the energy you work with. Because of their associations (see below), Wednesday and Thursday are the best days to work travel magic.

Generally, make sure that the planets and zodiac signs below support your magic. You can find the placements for a given time and place at the website Astrodienst; use the birth chart creation section for the date, location, and time you plan to perform the spell.[15]

Sun

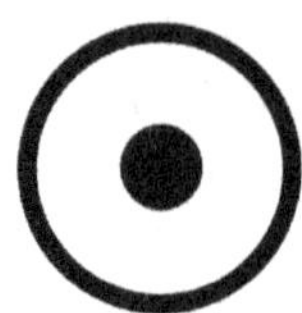

Day	Sunday
Zodiac Sign(s)	Aries, Cancer, Leo
Animals	Baboon, bee, bull, butterfly, chameleon, condor, crane, crow, cuckoo, deer, eagle, falcon, goat, hawk, hedgehog, hummingbird, jaguar, lion, lizard, monkey, parrot, peacock, raven, rooster, sheep, sparrow, swallow, swan, wolf, wren
Colors	Gold, orange, yellow
Plants	Acacia, angelica, ash, bamboo, birch, broom, carnation, cedar, chamomile, chrysanthemum, cinnamon, clove, corn, daffodil, daisy, eyebright, frankincense, galangal, ginseng, goldenseal, gorse, hazel, heliotrope, horse chestnut, juniper, laurel, linden, lovage, marigold, neroli, oak, olive, palm, peony, rosemary, rowan, St. John's wort, saffron, sunflower, walnut, witch hazel

15 www.astro.com/horoscope.

Stones	Amber, ametrine, beryl (golden), calcite (orange, red), carnelian, chrysoberyl, citrine, diamond, Herkimer diamond, peridot, quartz, ruby, sunstone, tiger's eye, topaz, tourmaline (black), zircon
Domains	Accomplishment, enlightenment, happiness, healing, optimism, pleasure, success, truth

MERCURY

Day	Wednesday
Zodiac Sign(s)	Gemini, Virgo
Animals	Blue jay, coyote, fox, jackal
Colors	Gray, green, purple, silver, yellow
Plants	Acacia, agrimony, ash, aspen, benzoin, bergamot, cedar, cherry, clary sage, clover, dill, elder, eucalyptus, fennel, hazel, honeysuckle, jasmine, juniper, lavender, lilac, linden, marjoram, peppermint, periwinkle, pomegranate, olive, pomegranate, rosemary, sage, valerian
Stones	Amber, aventurine, blue lace agate, carnelian, cat's eye, citrine, fluorite, hematite, jasper, moss agate, onyx, opal, peridot, rhodochrosite, sardonyx, sodalite, sphene, topaz
Domains	Adaptability, change(s), communication, creativity, curiosity, healing, hyperactivity, intellect, intelligence, land and air travel, language, learning, mathematics, memory, messages, public speaking, publishing, vehicles, and versatility

VENUS

Day	Friday
Zodiac Sign(s)	Taurus, Libra
Animals	Bull, dove, hare, lynx, raven, swan
Colors	Green, pink
Plants	Alder, aloe, apple, aspen, aster, basil, bergamot, birch, burdock, cardamom, catnip, cherry, columbine, coltsfoot, cowslip, daffodil, daisy, dittany, elder, feverfew, foxglove, geranium, goldenrod, heather, hibiscus, hyacinth, iris, Lady's Mantle, lilac, magnolia, mugwort, myrtle, orris root, passionflower, periwinkle, primrose, raspberry, rose, sandalwood, spearmint, strawberry, sycamore, thyme, valerian, vanilla, vervain, violet, willow, yarrow
Stones	Alexandrite, aventurine, azurite, calcite, carnelian, cat's eye, celestite, chrysoberyl, chrysocolla, chrysoprase, coral, desert rose, diamond dioptase, emerald, jade, jasper (green), kunzite, lapis lazuli, lodestone, malachite, mother-of-pearl, pearl, peridot, rhodochrosite, rose quartz, sapphire, sodalite, tourmaline (blue, green, pink, watermelon), tsavorite, turquoise
Domains	Affection, agriculture, astral realm, attraction, beauty, beginnings, compassion, connections, creativity, desire, emotions, energy (receptive, sexual), fertility, friendship, gentleness, happiness, harmony, kindness, love, lust, magic (sex), needs, passion, pleasure, rebirth/renewal, relationships, reversal, romance, sensuality, sex/sexuality, stress, unity

MOON

Day	Monday
Zodiac Sign(s)	Cancer
Animals	Bear, cat, cattle, crab, crane, crocodile, crow, cuckoo, dog, dolphin, elephant, fox, frog, goat, hare, hedgehog, heron, horse, ibis, jaguar, leopard, meadowlark, moth, nightingale, osprey, otter, owl, panther, peacock, pig (sow), rabbit, reindeer, seal, snail, snake, sparrow, spider, tiger, toad, tortoise, turtle
Colors	White, gray, silver
Plants	Aloe, bergamot, birch, gardenia, grape, iris, jasmine, lemon balm, lily, lotus, mesquite, myrrh, nutmeg, olive, palm, poppy, rosemary, rowan, saffron, sandalwood, willow
Stones	Abalone, agate, angelite, aquamarine, beryl, calcite (clear), Herkimer diamond, moonstone, morganite, mother-of-pearl, opal, quartz, sapphire, selenite, turquoise
Domains	Agriculture, animals, beginnings, change(s), consciousness (and subconscious), creativity, cycles, darkness, death, divination, dream work, emotions, enchantment, endings, energy (general, receptive), family, fertility, growth, guidance, healing, the home, imagination, inspiration, intuition, jealousy, life (rhythms), loneliness, love, magic, manifestation, moods, negativity, nightmares, obstacles, peace, power, pregnancy/childbirth, protection, psychic ability, rebirth/renewal, secrets, self-work, sensitivity, sorrow, spirits, transformation, wisdom

Each lunar month when the Moon is in Gemini is a good time for all magic regarding communication, public relations, moving house, and travel. Similarly, when the Moon is in Sagittarius, each lunar month is an opportune time to work magic for publications, legal matters, travel, and revealing truth.

MARS

Day	Tuesday
Zodiac Sign(s)	Aries, Sagittarius, Scorpio
Animals	Wolf
Colors	Red
Plants	Ash, basil, cherry, coriander, ginger, laurel, nasturtium, oak, rue, vervain
Stones	Bloodstone, carnelian, flint, garnet, hematite, jasper (red), lava, moldavite, onyx, pyrite, rhodochrosite, ruby, sardonyx, tourmaline (red and watermelon)
Domains	Action, aggression, anger, assertiveness, battle/war, beginnings, courage, death, defense, desire, determination, emotions, endurance, energy (sexual), enmity, growth, justice, life, lust, magic (general, defensive, sex), passion, power, sex/sexuality (male), skills, strength, willpower

JUPITER

Day	Thursday
Zodiac Sign(s)	Sagittarius, Pisces
Animals	Deer, eagle, unicorn
Colors	Light green, blue, purple
Plants	Agrimony, aloe, anise, betony, birch, borage, cedar, chestnut, cinquefoil, clove, fir, honeysuckle, horse chestnut, lemon balm, linden, magnolia, maple, meadowsweet, myrrh, nutmeg, oak, oakmoss, olive, pine, sage, star anise, sycamore, walnut, yew
Stones	Amethyst, lepidolite, sugilite, turquoise, zircon (red)
Domains	Abundance, authority, business, charity, control, dignity, discipline, expansion, friendships, gambling, generosity, higher education, honor, influence, justice, leadership, luck, material wealth, opportunities, optimism, philosophy, power, pride, problems, prosperity, publishing, religion, responsibility, spirituality, sports, success, traveling abroad, and all long journeys

SATURN

Day	Saturday
Zodiac Sign(s)	Aquarius, Capricorn, Libra
Animals	Bee, crow, donkey, goat, raven, wren
Colors	Black, blue (navy), brown, gray (dark), green (dark), yellow
Plants	Amaranth, aspen, beech, belladonna, bittersweet, blackthorn, carnation, comfrey, cypress, elm, fir, holly, ivy, lady's slipper, magnolia, mandrake, mesquite, mimosa, monkshood, morning glory, mullein, myrrh, patchouli, pine, poplar, rowan, rue, skullcap, Solomon's seal, witch hazel, yew
Stones	Apache tears, azurite, carnelian, hematite, jasper (brown), jet, obsidian, onyx, sapphire, sardonyx, serpentine, tourmaline (black)
Domains	Agriculture, ambition, astral realm, authority, banish, bind, business, concentration/focus, darkness, death, discipline, endings, endurance, freedom, goals, grounding, justice, karma, knowledge, limitations/boundaries, longevity, loyalty, lust, the mind, obstacles, peace, purification, relationships, stability, strength

URANUS

Day	None
Zodiac Sign(s)	Aquarius, Gemini
Animals	None
Colors	Indigo, yellow
Plants	Ash, rowan
Stones	Amazonite, aventurine, Herkimer diamond, labradorite, quartz
Domains	Ambition, anger, change(s), community, cooperation, freedom, goals, hope, illumination, improvement, intuition, motivation, power, relationships

Neptune

Day	None
Zodiac Sign(s)	Aquarius, Pisces
Animals	Fish, crustaceans, octopus, squid
Colors	Sea green, lavender, purple
Plants	Ash, lotus, jasmine, mulberry (white), ferns, moss, sea anemone, seaweed, water lily, willow
Stones	Amethyst, angelite, aquamarine, beryl, celestite, coral, fluorite, jade, labradorite, lapis lazuli, lepidolite, mother-of-pearl, sapphire, turquoise
Domains	Awareness (expanding), clairvoyance, community, consciousness (subconscious), creativity, dream work, enchantment, energy (psychic), guardian, guidance, inspiration, intuition, life, the Otherworld, power, protection, psychic ability, sensitivity, visions

Pluto

Day	None
Zodiac Sign(s)	Cancer, Scorpio
Animals	Eagle, fox, barn owl, scorpion, snake
Colors	Black, brown, crimson, maroon
Plants	Basil, belladonna, bittersweet, chrysanthemum, cypress, fern, foxglove, hemlock, nettle, pomegranate, poppies, reed, rhododendron, rosemary, vanilla

Stones	Amethyst, garnet, jet, kunzite, labradorite, obsidian, quartz (tourmalinated), spinel, tourmaline
Domains	The afterlife, change(s), danger, darkness (inner), death, dream work, justice, karma, memory/memories, the Otherworld/Underworld, rebirth/renewal, secrets, sex/sexuality, spirituality, transformation, wealth

The Third House rules local travel and communications. If your spell involves local travel or communication, check what is in this house, as well as the placement of the planet Mercury, particularly as it relates to the Zodiac sign Gemini.

The Ninth House rules long-distance travel and learning about/understanding the world. If your spell concerns long-distance travel or any aspect of learning about and understanding your world, check what planets are in the Ninth House, as well as the placement of the planet Jupiter, particularly as it relates to the zodiac sign of Sagittarius.

SEASONS

Sometimes you want to work with the energy of an entire season. The following are the most common correspondences for each of them:

- **Spring:** Air, all baby creatures, amethyst, anise, aquamarine, butterfly, chamomile, daffodil, green, hibiscus, hyssop, iris, lemongrass, marjoram, moonstone, myrtle, pastel (colors), pennyroyal, primrose, robin, rose quartz, rosemary, spikenard, star anise, white, wild lettuce, yellow
- **Summer:** Acacia, allspice, basil, bay leaf (laurel), bee, calendula, camphor, carnelian, catnip, cinnamon, citrine, clove, dragon's blood, dragonfly, eagle, emerald, fire, garnet, ginger, gold, hawk, honey, hops, horehound, horse, jade, lavender, lemon, mint, orange, patchouli, red, rose, ruby, sage, sunflower, turmeric, wren
- **Autumn:** Aloeswood, apples, aventurine, brown, cinnamon, citrine, coltsfoot, corn, gold, goldenseal, Irish moss, maple, myrrh, oakmoss,

owl, pinecone, pumpkin, red cedar, rose hips, saffron, salmon, sandalwood, squash, squirrel, stag, tarragon, thyme, tiger's eye, water, yarrow

- **Winter:** Amber, bloodstone, calamus, cardamom, cedar, clove, diamond, earth, eucalyptus, evergreens, fox, frankincense, goose, juniper, mistletoe, mugwort, nutmeg, owl, peppermint, peridot, pine, reindeer, rosemary, ruby, sandalwood, stag, valerian, vetiver, woodruff, yew

Stone Allies

Stones have long been a Witch's ally in augmenting and directing their magic. For the traveler, carrying an extra boost can make all the difference in the world. You can program your stones for energy, guidance, protection...anything you might find helpful. Even better, stones are so easy to tuck into a pocket and tough enough to survive being repeatedly handled; unlike paper, they are excellent for carrying through a long journey.

Many stones are associated with the days of the week, planets, seasons, and plant allies you might work with for travel magic. The below collection represents the ones most directly tied to travel. As always, add your own!

- **Crystal Quartz:** If you can only have one stone, I recommend crystal quartz. Like white candles, clear quartz is an all-around helpful stone. It can be programmed with any intent, holding energy until needed. It has a direct connection to Water and matters regarding communication. When attached to a cord or chain, it makes an excellent pendulum for divination. Wear or carry a piece of quartz as protection against the elements and general mayhem.
- **Amethyst:** A potent and protective stone, it is one I recommend be included in every Witch's collection. It guards against psychic attacks and naturally acts as a calmer if you hold it in your receptive hand and take several deep, slow breaths. Amethyst has substantial

healing and cleansing powers, helping the wearer feel less scattered, more focused, and in control. It facilitates decision-making, bringing common sense and dispelling anger, rage, fear, and anxiety.

- **Aquamarine:** A stone for courage, aquamarine calms the mind and soothes stress. Ancient sailors carried it as a ward against drowning. It brings closure to ongoing situations and clarity to blocked communications. Packing this stone, tucked into a side pocket, can help guard against storms; fishermen often use it as an amulet against danger.
- **Beryl:** Associated with the sea, beryl is an outstanding stone for dealing with stress, reducing fear, and promoting a positive outlook. If lost, hold a piece of beryl in your receptive hand and visualize where you need to be, then follow your intuition.
- **Carnelian:** A fiercely protective stone, carnelian promotes peace, pleasure, and prosperity, bringing joy to those going on a long journey or moving house. It protects travelers and public speakers by bolstering self-confidence and courage.
- **Chalcedony:** Excellent at banishing fear, chalcedony attracts public favor, recognition, and financial reward, and increases popularity, enthusiasm, and fitness.
- **Coral:** Technically the skeletal remains of a sea creature, coral offers a direct connection to the sea. Most potent when it is in its natural state, not worked by human hands, coral is fiercely protective. It helps dispel foolishness and poor decision-making, as well as guarding against accidents and theft.
- **Emerald:** A favorite when working in matters of love, emerald assists with eloquent speech, inspires confidence, and increases understanding. Strongly protective, ancient travelers often bound one to their left arm for the duration of the journey.
- **Garnet:** Another protective stone (particularly against thieves), garnet can be tapped to boost physical energy, such as when hiking. It also helps maintain one's humor under challenging circumstances and protects travelers from injury and contagious disease.
- **Jasper:** Stimulating mental alertness and awareness, all forms of jasper protect against physical and non-physical threats. Specific colors have additional properties:

- **Brown:** Connects the wearer to the earth, offering endurance and strength.
- **Green:** Accelerates healing.
- **Mottle:** Protection against drowning.
- **Red:** Sends harm back to the caster.
- **Lapis Lazuli:** This beautiful blue stone is distinguished from sodalite (which has veins of white) by the veins of pyrite (gold) running through it. It is a healing stone, improving mental, physical, and emotional states. Inspiring confidence and courage, it helps the wearer to succeed, anywhere.
- **Moonstone:** Use moonstone for general protection when traveling as it connects the wearer with the Moon's journey through the zodiac each month. Sailors have long worn moonstone rings to protect them on the water.
- **Petrified Wood:** Another product of a living creature, this fossil deflects negative energy and protects against drowning. May also endow the holder with endurance and longevity.
- **Sapphire:** Superb for promoting positive social interaction and enhancing wisdom. It protects the wearer from negativity and banishes fraud.
- **Tiger's Eye:** Scott Cunningham reports that Roman soldiers wore this stone during battle; its protective powers against all forms of danger are significant. Supporting courage and a sense of conviction, this is a wonderful stone for the traveler who needs extra help to get out of a jam.
- **Turquoise:** Often used in jewelry, turquoise is carried as a stone of protection against negativity and bad luck. It promotes courage and protects against disease, accidents, violence, and poison. It is an all-around good stone for travelers.

Cards: Playing and Tarot

I always travel with a deck of cards; they are a great way to pass the time. Some of those cards also offer a boost for your travel magic. All cards, whether playing or Tarot, offer many opportunities for divination.

It was so freaking late and we were beyond jet-lagged, having entered some alternate universe where neither of us had slept for twenty-seven hours. The airport concessions were closed, and we had hours until our next flight boarded. "Do we try to get a room and some sleep?" my husband wondered.

"Or food?" I replied. Then we just looked at each other, neither wanting to make a decision that might end with our missing the connection, the one that would finally get us home finally. I pulled out my deck of cards, and we moved to a corner of the gate. Shuffling the deck three times, I asked, "Will all turn out well if we get a hotel room now?" and pulled the Six of Diamonds. "Come on, sweetie, let's get a room."

Right outside was a lovely modern hotel with a spare room for cheap and twenty-four-hour room service. My phone buzzed just before we put the tray with the remains from our excellent omelet with fries in the hall to be taken away. It was the airline; our early morning plane had been canceled, and we were re-booked on a later flight. Happily, with thanks to the universe, we reset our alarm and got a good night's sleep.

Quick Card Charm

This is a favorite card charm of mine. You will need:

- Deck of playing cards
- Paper
- Pen

Take three deep breaths and center yourself. Choose the card that best represents your need (this can be through intuition, random choice, or using the tables provided). Recreate the chosen card on the paper, then write out your need over the images you first drew. As you do, concentrate on your need and what you want to happen. When finished, say out loud: "*As I will, so mote it be!*" Wrap the paper and tuck it into your pocket. Replace the card in the deck.

Yes/No Card Reading

Much travel involves quick decision-making. This is a technique I developed from a similar one I use with my Tarot cards. You will need:

- Deck of playing cards

Take three deep breaths and center yourself. Carefully consider your yes/no question; what will give you the most information? You might ask:

Will I make my connection?
Will this journey bring me joy?
Is this boat/vehicle/plane safe?

Shuffle your cards at least three times, but no more than nine, while keeping your attention on your question (I like to repeat the question with each card blend). Then, choose a single card. Over the years, these are the meanings I have come to associate when using playing cards for this yes/no divination.

Number	Meaning
Ace	Yes!
Two	No, more plans or information are needed
Three	Yes, but you'll need patience
Four	Yes
Five	No, something needs to happen first
Six	Yes!
Seven	Maybe
Eight	Yes!
Nine	Yes, but take it easy (be cautious)
Ten	No! Wait for a better situation/opportunity
Jack	Yes, if it's safe; no, if there is any risk involved

Number	Meaning
Queen	Yes
King	Yes, if you feel like you have all of the information

CARD MEANINGS

In general, the four suits of playing cards relate to the Tarot suits, although the linkage is only sometimes clear.

Playing Card	Tarot Suit(s)	Meaning
Diamonds	Pentacles, Disks, Coins	Money, practical matters, Earth
Clubs	Wands, Rods, Staves	Creativity, action, Fire
Hearts	Cups	Emotions, relationships, Water
Spades	Swords	Thinking, communication, conflict, Air

The numbered cards clearly align.

Number	Positive Meaning	Negative Meaning
Ace	Beginnings, a fresh start, new	None (Aces are always positive)
Two	Balance, choice, decisions, planning, preparation	Waiting, juggling resources, failed communication
Three	Connections, joy, exploration	Division, mixed communication, plans gone awry
Four	Stability, recovery	Being stuck, delays, going nowhere
Five	Challenges, competition	Disturbance, loss, despair, disagreement
Six	Harmony, victory, travel, nostalgia, resources	Dissonance
Seven	Organization, details	Distractions, theft, dissatisfaction

Number	Positive Meaning	Negative Meaning
Eight	Movement	Stagnation, lack of movement, imbalance
Nine	Growth	Satiety, indulgence, battles, worry
Ten	Completion, Achievement of goals	Unfinished business

The court cards are the most apparent difference between playing cards and Tarot decks. If your deck includes the Joker (mine doesn't), it is similar to the Fool card of the Tarot. The Joker represents taking risks, acting foolishly, or getting into an unexpected situation through innocence.

Looking at the table, the Ace of Hearts might indicate a new relationship or friendship, the Three of Clubs exploration, and the Nine of Spades problems and worry.

Playing Card Layout: Three Card

If there is time, you can do a more elaborate reading to get more information about your situation.

Three cards laid out left to right are one of the most popular layouts. The left card represents the influences affecting the current situation, the center card indicates the current situation, and the card to the right signifies the future if you make no changes.

Typical Three-Card Layout

Other three-card layouts I suggest are:

- Current situation (left), the obstacle (center), and advice offered (right)
- What you can change (left), what you can't change (center), and what you may not be aware of (right)
- The nature of your problem (left), the reason for the problem (center), and a potential solution (right)

Travel-Specific Tarot Cards

Several cards found in many Tarot decks have travel-specific connections. They are most valuable when doing spellwork or in Tarot readings because bringing a Tarot deck takes up valuable space in my suitcase.

- **The Chariot** talks about the drive of the querent and whether those sphinxes are leading them to victory or defeat. This is a valuable card for protection during road trips and all travel by car.
- **The World** indicates the successful completion of the cycle. It's excellent for protection during international travel.
- **King of Pentacles** promises a great deal of travel, which is perfect for spellwork to bring into your life.
- **Queen of Wands** offers opportunities to develop a project involving travel or a new career either by taking a leadership role or increasing your financial security.
- **Knight of Wands** is perfect for a spell to manifest a vacation; make sure your request for time off gets approved, or find backup during your time away.
- **Knight of Swords** represents travel by air; use it for protection when you fly.

- **Eight of Wands** is a movement, advancement, and expansion card. It represents travel to a faraway place, usually by air.
- **Eight of Cups** indicates embarking on a journey, leaving one's home base well-protected and supplied.
- **Six of Swords** represents a trip by boat; use it for protection when you are on the water.
- **Three of Wands** suggests expansion in different directions and indicates that travel might be required.

Chapter Three

Preparing for Travel

I've always held the belief that physical setting can play a significant role in one's magical practice, serving as both a catalyst and inspiration. What does this mean, exactly? The concept of location in your practice entails the deliberate positioning of your magical workings. It may involve simple considerations, such as finding the ideal spot in your home for your altar or selecting a suitable location in your town to bury a charm. On the other hand, it can also involve more intricate arrangements and choices regarding the placement of magical workings.

Let's say, for instance, that your beloved grandmother held a special place in your heart and she recently passed away. You want to perform a blessing for her spirit's journey and provide solace to those left behind. Is it sufficient to conduct this ritual in the confines of your grandmother's home? Perhaps she maintained a deep connection to her ancestral homeland, prompting you to embark on a journey with her ashes (or a symbolic token) to bring her peace in her native land. Alternatively, it could be as uncomplicated as visiting her cherished spot, even if it appears ordinary. Although my grandfather's favorite haunt was the bowling alley, which may not seem inherently sacred, it would hold significant significance if I aimed to create a spell to console his departing spirit.

As for location being a prompt for your practice, this is a bit more esoteric. My husband and I trace our ancestries back at least partially to the British Isles. In our personal journey, my husband and I have discovered ancestral roots intertwined with the British Isles. This revelation has shaped our travels, with a particular focus on Scotland and Ireland, where we embarked on a sacred quest to explore ancient sites. Another compelling example lies in the heart of my spiritual devotion, which is deeply rooted in the Greek pantheon. Although

I didn't set out to be a devotee of the Hellenic gods, their presence found me, guiding my path. As the opportunity arose to plan our next adventure, an irresistible call beckoned me to venture into the storied lands of Greece, seeking profound connections with my spirituality. The world brims with captivating destinations and, though we may never visit them all, our spiritual path can illuminate the way, directing us toward meaningful destinations and purposeful experiences.

Magic as Locational Prompt

As I mentioned earlier, my husband and I have used our travel to explore our spirituality on numerous occasions. My previously agnostic partner has been swayed towards his spiritual path in no small part by visiting so many places held sacred by humans for millennia. We once visited Newgrange, a site in Ireland aligned with the Winter Solstice so that a sacred space buried deep within an artificial hill receives direct light through a space in the lintel in the early morning of the solstice. The outside of the place is beautiful, its earthworks adorned with a wall of white stones.[16] His primary takeaway from Newgrange was not the beauty of the site or the astronomical alignment of it, but the sheer act of faith that building it required. As he puts it, "Research indicates that Newgrange was constructed over at least thirty years, maybe as many as one hundred. Given the lifespans of that era, not only were there people who conceived of the place knowing that they'd probably never see it completed, there were people born not having been a part of the conception and still not certain that they'd see it finished, who nevertheless contributed to its construction. I can barely grasp that kind of communal faith."

Regardless of the path you tread, the tapestry of locations on this planet carries profound connections to its origins and ongoing narrative. Even for those who approach their practice with a logical lens, delving into the teachings and origins of renowned schools of

16 Yes, I'm aware that the site has been restored. Still, to the best of my knowledge, the restoration was done as faithfully as possible and helped immeasurably by observing similar nearby sites that have yet to be disturbed at all.

thought or philosophical frameworks can unveil captivating destinations. If your faith encompasses deity worship or cultural customs, the tapestry of meaningful places awaiting your exploration expands even further. This becomes particularly relevant when you find yourself drawn to a culture that may not be rooted in your own ancestral heritage. As we have explored earlier, cultural appropriation remains a genuine concern in our world. Navigating the fine line between respectfully continuing traditions and extracting them from their meaningful context can be a delicate task. There's no such thing as doing "too much" homework in learning about the practices you follow and visiting their ancestral home(s) can only be to the good, enriching your connection and deepening your appreciation.

Deciding where to go can be tricky, depending on what you're trying to accomplish; it's harder to investigate some places than others. As we were planning our trip to Greece, you won't be surprised to hear that we got completely overwhelmed by the many options available. Should we look for deity-specific sites? Focus on archeological wonders? Dive deep into one specific region? Ultimately, we prioritized sites that were truly important to us, regardless of how famous they might be. That's why we found ourselves wandering the rural back roads of the island of Naxos, looking for a Temple of Demeter. We failed, despite excellent pictures, government-issued signposts, and up-to-date mapping technology. We're still unsure whether we failed a test Demeter set us to, if Mercury introduced some chaos as a well-deserved lesson, or if we just got lost.

In any case, if we count the sheer number of devotees, the seven most sacred places on Earth are:

- **Jerusalem:** Significantly spiritual for three of the world's most prominent religions—Judaism, Christianity, and Islam.
- **Kashi Vishwanath Temple, Varanasi, Uttar Pradesh, India:** A Jyotirlinga shrine dedicated to Lord Shiva, to which Hindu devotees are expected to travel at least once in their lifetimes.
- **Lourdes, France:** A place of Catholic pilgrimage.

- **Mahabodhi Temple, Bodh Gaya, Bihar:** Site where Prince Siddhartha gained Enlightenment and became Gautama Buddha. It is the most sacred place of pilgrimage for Buddhists in the world.
- **Mecca, Saudi Arabia:** The center of the Islam world, the direction toward which all face when praying. Non-Islamic people may not enter the inner precincts.
- **Uluru-Kata Tjuta National Park, Australia:** Sacred to Aboriginal people for thousands of years.
- **Mount Sinai, Egypt:** Significantly sacred to the Jewish, Christian, and Islamic faiths.[17]

There are, however, many more sites you might visit in a nearly overwhelming variety. In addition to Paleolithic and Neolithic sacred sites, there are thousands of places venerated by the historical religions of Judaism, Christianity, Hinduism, Jainism, Buddhism, Shintoism, Taoism, Islam, Sikhism, and Zoroasterism. Sites used by Pagans in pre-Gardnerian practice are scattered about the entire planet. Sacred places are found at naturally occurring geological features, such as caves, mountains, forest glens, springs, and waterfalls. Others are created through human-made ceremonial structures such as pyramids, stone rings, temples, mosques, shrines, and cathedrals.

The sheer variety may make one wonder: what makes a place sacred? Many perspectives, such as academia, travel writers, and personal experiences, define many answers. One answer is that sacred places are those places that offer the potential for a mystical experience. For whatever reason, the location facilitates the possibility of being in contact with the intangible.

---

17 Note that many scholars question whether the biblical Mount Sinai has indeed been discovered. Still, most religious personages agree that it is presently known as Jabal Musa on the Sinai Peninsula.

Sacred Places of the World

As much as we want it to, visiting a place that many call sacred will not automatically create a transcendental experience (Stonehenge was simply a great collection of rocks for me). At the same time, we can have such an experience at some location that doesn't otherwise have anything we might call mystical about it.

Here is a collection to jumpstart your research:

Africa

- Bet Giyorgis, Ethiopia
- Abu Simbel Temples, Nubia, Egypt
- Pyramids of Gizah, Egypt
- Holy City of Zerhoun, Morocco
- Cave art sites of Tassili n' Ajjer, Algeria
- Tsodilo Hills Cave Paintings, Botswana

The Americas

- Vortexes, Sedona, Arizona, United States
- Cenote Sagrado, Chichen Itza, Mexico
- Basilica of Our Lady of Guadalupe, Mexico City
- Lake Atitlan, Guatemala
- Lake Titicaca, border of Peru and Bolivia
- Devils Tower, Wyoming, United States
- Great Sandhills, Saskatchewan, Canada
- Writing-on-Stone, Lethbridge, Alberta, Canada
- Moose Mountain, Saskatchewan, Canada
- Petroglyph Park, Vancouver Island, British Columbia, Canada
- Peterborough Petroglyphs, southern Ontario, Canada
- Chichen Itza, Yucatan, Mexico
- Teotihuacan, State of Mexico, Mexico
- Tula, Hidalgo, Mexico
- Tulum, Yucatan, Mexico

- Uxmal, Yucatan, Mexico
- Mt. St. Elias, Alaska, United States
- Enchanted Rock, Texas, United States
- Mt. Taylor, New Mexico, United States
- Zuni Lake, Arizona, United States
- Mt. Kilauea, Hawaii, United States

ASIA

- Shwedagon Pagoda, Myanmar
- Lotus Temple, New Delhi, India
- Boudhanath, Nepal
- Harmandir Sahib (popularly known as Golden Temple), Amritsar, India
- Thiksey Monastery, India
- Char Dham, Uttarakhand, India (this is a circuit of four places: Gangotri, dedicated to River Goddess Ganga; Yamunotri, dedicated to River Goddess Yamuna; Badrinath, dedicated to Lord Badri (Vishnu); and Kedarnath, dedicated to Lord Shiva)
- Jagannath Temple, Puri, India
- Amarnath Cave, India
- Borobudur, Indonesia
- Batu Caves, Malaysia
- Basilica of Bom Jesus, Goa, India
- Angkor Wat, Cambodia
- Naritasan Shinshoji Temple, Japan
- Tirupati, India
- Dwarka, India
- Jokhang Temple, Lhasa, Tibet
- Koyasan, Japan
- Tiger's Nest Monastery in Paro, Bhutan

Europe

- Spanish Synagogue, Czech Republic
- St. Peter's Basilica, Vatican City
- Glastonbury Tor, England
- Saint-Michel d'Aiguilhe Chapel, France
- Meteora, Greece
- Basilica of San Vitale, Italy
- Shrine of Padre Pio, San Giovanni Rotondo, Italy
- Mount Parnassus, Greece
- Notre Dame Cathedral, Paris
- Cologne Cathedral, Cologne, Germany
- Basilica De Sagrada Familia, Spain
- Westminster Abbey, London
- Hill of Crosses, Lithuania
- Medjugorje in Bosnia and Herzegovina
- Montserrat, Spain
- Mount Saint Michel, France
- Newgrange, Boyne Valley, Ireland
- St. Brigid's Cathedral and Perpetual Flame, Kildare Ireland
- Sanctuary of Fatima, Portugal
- Santiago de Composte, Spain
- Walsingham, United Kingdom
- Stonehenge, United Kingdom
- Drombeg Stone Circle, Glandore, Ireland
- Avebury Plain, United Kingdom
- Callanish Stones, Isle of Lewis, United Kingdom
- Skara Brae, Orkney, Scotland, United Kingdom
- Megalithic Temples, Malta
- Ğgantija Temple Complex, Malta
- Khirokitia, Cyprus
- Akrotiri, Santorini, Greece

MIDDLE EAST

- Hagia Sophia, Istanbul, Turkey
- Sultan Ahmed Mosque, Turkey
- Baha'i Shrine and Gardens, Haifa, Israel
- Garden Tomb, Jerusalem (believed to be the site of Jesus' burial and resurrection from the dead)
- Nasir al-Mulk Mosque, Shiraz, Iran
- The Church of the Nativity, Bethlehem, Palestine
- Göbeklitepe, Turkey
- Bir Hima, Saudi Arabia

I am aware of one undeniable truth: every country in the world holds its own sacred places. So, I ask you, dear reader, where is the sacred site nearest to you at this very moment?

OFFERINGS AT SACRED SITES

Over the years, I have been to places where the sacred energy is almost palpable, available to any visitor with the smallest amount of psychic ability. In every single one of those places, someone before me had left an offering. Even if the site is practically unmarked and known only to those who went looking, inevitably, I've found items left by others, including coins, ribbon-wrapped flowers, seashells, lengths of fabric, and small toys.

Don't do that.

Seriously, please don't.

I promise you that the being of such a place—the *locus genii,* if you will—has absolutely no use for whatever you are leaving behind, even if it's "environmentally friendly." Glass candle holders, crystals, non-native food items...they may seem like they would be acceptable to use, but they are all as bad as plastic and other nonbiodegradable items. Even if your offering is biodegradable (like food), the decomposition process still takes years (decades in many cases) and alters the ecosystem.

When you leave those offerings, as well-intentioned as you may be, you harm the place and the natural creatures that inhabit the space. Your food offering (unless you are 100% sure beyond any shadow of a doubt, as in, you've done more research than just an online search) may teach a local creature to expect food from humans, making them less afraid to approach, leading to attacks. It may be poisonous. Are you sure your libation won't kill the native flora? Don't tie things to trees or bushes—so-called "clootie trees" are probably an ancient custom, but when hundreds of people do it, the harm caused is enormous. Bringing non-native plants or other items can grant invasive species a place within an otherwise secure ecosystem. Wine is a corrosive agent, as is the metal from coins.

For years, our books and teachers told us, "Leave an offering as thanks for taking a cutting from the plant—or taking anything (even a sense of quiet)—from a sacred space." They meant well; truly, they did. But when many humans (not just a few) engage in an activity, it turns to harm rather than health.

Instead, I urge you to take the attitude of leaving nothing behind you when you go. Even better, make your offering one of service and take the trash you find there when you go. It's a lot more nature-friendly and likely to be viewed with active favor by the *locus genii.*

The most potent offerings come from us personally, such as a snippet (not a lock) of our hair,[18] a song, or a few drops of our saliva. Pure water is safe and acceptable if you absolutely must leave something not of yourself.

To make an offering, settle near the place you feel is most suitable. Take a few moments to introduce yourself to the area, either out loud or in your mind. Clearly state who you are and why you are there; you are reaching out and forming a relationship, which necessitates respect and patience. Listen for a reply, although it may not come until later, in your dreams or in some fashion unexpected. When you feel

18 I used to think hair was okay, but it turns out that birds and other small animals can choke on it, or the strands can wrap around vegetation and kill it. Taking a tiny snip of your hair, no more than a few millimeters (or 1/8") long is probably okay. Alternatively, use loose/collected eyelashes or eyebrow hair.

enough time has passed, thank the area for its attention and energy and make your offering. Leave with respect.

And for the love of all that's holy, stop rearranging the rocks.

Talking to the Divine

Obtaining guidance through divination is an ability every Witch can tap into, and doing so while planning your journey is wise. The best tools for me are the pendulum and Tarot cards, but you might prefer to work through dreams, oracle cards, astrology, runes, or some other method. Knowing what technique works best for you is what is essential.

Pendulum

If you aren't familiar with the pendulum, you might be surprised by how versatile this divinatory tool is and how long humans have used it to communicate with the Divine. While some link it to the Oracle at Delphi, Galileo first noted (circa 1583) the constancy of a pendulum's movement by comparing a swinging lamp with his pulse rate. Based on that, nearly a century later, the mathematician Huygens invented a clock controlled by a pendulum, thus creating the standard of timekeeping for almost three hundred years. Ordinary people have been (provably) using pendulums (often in the form of a forked stock) to dowse for water, gold, oil, and missing items since at least the time of Galileo.[19]

A pendulum is a weighted, well-balanced object suspended from a cord or chain, commonly made from metal or semi-precious stone. Some use a favorite piece of jewelry, such as a wedding ring or pendant; I've used pieces of rock from a specific place, acorns, and seashells. In a pinch, almost anything can do; as I discussed in Chapter Two: Correspondences, creating sympathies in your magic can assist you.

19 St. Teresa of Spain was offered a site for a convent that lacked water. A friar in her retinue dowsed for water after making the sign of the cross and indicated a place to dig. When they did so, water poured forth (Barrett 171).

Pendulums respond to the energetic connection between your physical body, your higher self, and your relationship to deity or your subconscious. This connection creates small movements in your arm and wrist that cause the pendulum to move in specific ways, called the ideomotor reflex. When we ask a yes/no question, our energy field moves the pendulum according to the answers we receive. Some people have a prepared "board" to assist with reading the received messages. These boards—made of paper or fabric—often depict a cross within a circle, with the four divisions marked as yes/no and maybe/never. A more complex version contains all the letters of the alphabet and the numerals from zero to ten along a half-circle or arc. If you're picturing the Ouija boards of your youth, you've got the idea close enough.

Using a pendulum is simple. When you are just starting, it's best if the pendulum chain is relatively short, as reading the signals received on long chains is harder (you can remedy a too-long chain by looping it lightly around your index finger). Sit comfortably with your feet on the floor and relax your body. Take three deep breaths, clearing your mind. Carefully formulate your yes/no question.

When you have your question clearly in mind, hold the end of the pendulum string, chain, or cord between your thumb and forefinger in your dominant hand with the weighted part hanging down. Run your other hand down the length of the chain in a stroking motion, ending with your hand resting under the bottom tip of the pendulum, just touching your upturned palm. The pendulum starts to work from this place of complete stillness. Move your hand away from the bottom of the pendulum and observe how the pendulum starts moving.

Remain as relaxed as possible, allowing your energy to flow naturally, and watch the pendulum move so that your yes or no answer becomes clear. The answers may need to be clarified the first few times as your pendulum gets to know you. Don't ask more than three questions; keep them focused on a specific topic or area. As with most things, practice makes reading the answers much more apparent.

Some, me included, start each session with calibration when we aren't using a board. I hold my pendulum with no pertinent question in mind and say, "What is neutral?" Usually, the pendulum begins to move in small circles over my palm at that point. I then ask what Yes looks like, then No. The response is almost invariably the opposite movement—sideways vs. forward-and-backward or clockwise vs. counterclockwise—but check to be sure. Only after I see that do I proceed with my pertinent questions.

Anyone can use a pendulum if they have a bit of privacy (perhaps not in an airport waiting area). If you travel with it, I recommend wrapping it in some silk to protect it from picking up on external influences. If you're using a piece of jewelry (like a wedding ring), rinse it under water and dry it with silk to prepare it.

If the answers you receive do not make sense, it may mean one of three things: the question was not clearly phrased enough, the answer is not available, or you've overdone it or are too tired and need to take a rest. While not getting an answer is annoying, consider that it still provides information that we can use to act—or not—upon.

Responses I've heard from students regularly, particularly if they feel that they aren't getting an answer, often boil down to incredulity. "This isn't going to work; no deity is talking to me through a string!" And maybe they aren't. Earlier, when I mentioned both "deity or your subconscious" in Chapter Three: Pendulums, that wasn't just idle talk. Almost all of us are comfortable with some notion of divided consciousness, whether it's the classic "id/ego/superego" model, or simply consciousness vs. subconsciousness. Hearing directly from anything beyond your active consciousness takes some doing, and divination can be a relatively direct conduit to the other part of you. A skeptic will see pendulum divination and scoff that: "you're moving the string yourself." To use the scientific nomenclature for a moment, "no duh!" What they don't consider is *which part of myself is doing the moving?* Giving over control to the bit of your mind that you aren't actively directing is essentially receiving an answer from a mind that is not your moment-to-moment self. And, of course, for those of us who believe we are in a relationship with a deity, it is the most natural thing in the world to try to get out of the way so that deity can "pick up the pen," so to speak.

Tarot Cards

I've been using Tarot cards since my college days, going on four decades now, and they are my absolute go-to for divination. Tarot cards offer insight into the oft-unknown unconscious part of ourselves, access our native intuition, and open a conduit to the wisdom of deity. Using them to prepare for your trip or taking a deck with you is a great idea. Think about it this way: most of us travel to expand our knowledge of the world, learn more about ourselves, and escape from our comfort zone, all of which align well with Tarot readings. Tarot cards can guide us through difficult and stressful times, offering clarity when we feel most confused.

Every Tarot reading starts with a question. Imagine this: you're considering taking a vacation somewhere new, but you've been feeling slightly "off" and out-of-sorts lately. You might ask the cards how this trip will impact your emotions or if it will have a spiritual or physical effect on you. Knowing what the vacation might bring can help you prepare for what might come about. Consider the reason you are taking the trip; what do you most want to happen? For some, it's a time to reflect and consider our place within the larger world; for others, it's a chance to reconnect with our loved ones. Still others need to unplug and recharge their internal batteries so we can continue to take care of ourselves and others.

Three-Card Travel Layout

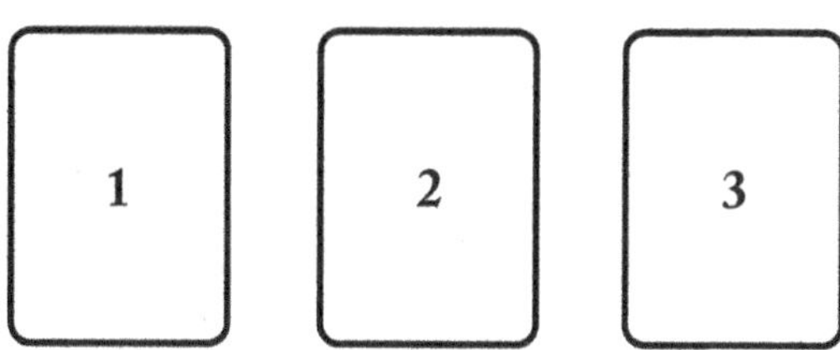

Any Tarot card can offer clarity for your journey, just as any layout offers insight. Besides asking a yes/no question with a single card, my preferred layout for travel-related readings uses three cards, reading from left to right.

A layout I often use early in my planning looks at options:

- **Card One:** Option one
- **Card Two:** Option two
- **Card Three:** Option three

Often followed by one that assists in decision-making:

- **Card One:** Option one
- **Card Two:** Option two
- **Card Three:** What I need to know to decide between the two

A variation of this looks at the coming journey on a deeper level and is one I often do the week before leaving:

- **Card One:** Opportunities
- **Card Two:** Challenges
- **Card Three:** What will come of the journey?

If I need guidance while traveling, I will often use this layout:

- **Card One:** Situation
- **Card Two:** Action needed
- **Card Three:** Outcome

A friend showed me a layout I also like to use while traveling:[20]

- **Card One:** What you *can* change
- **Card Two:** What you *can't* change
- **Card Three:** What you aren't aware of

Aside from a three-card reading, I like to use a specific five-card layout, which initially came from Benebell Wen.

20 Thanks, C.! (personal communication, 2005)

Five-Card Travel Layout

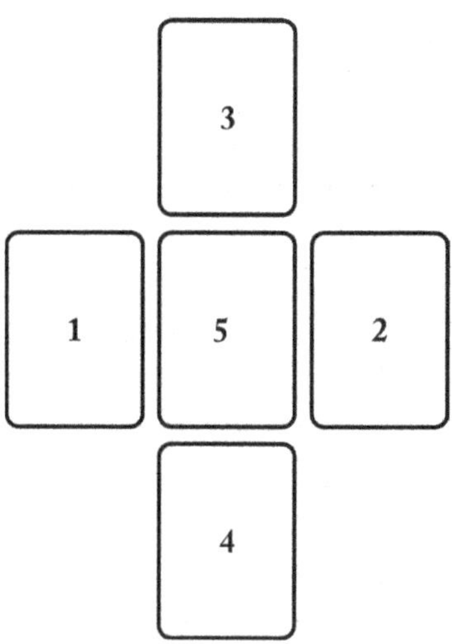

Wen approaches the reading a little differently than I do, preferring to ask a specific question with each card of the layout instead of a single question for the entire layout. For their spread, shuffle the cards and fan them out in an arc across the area in front of you. Contemplate the question for the first card, and draw a card, placing it in the number one position (see the image above). Reflect on its implications (you may want to record your thoughts in your journal). Repeat the second question below and draw a card, placing it in the number two position of the layout and spending time considering what the card is telling you. Continue through the remaining three cards, each in turn.

The five questions asked are:

- **Card One:** What will I get out of this trip?
- **Card Two:** What will I give because of this trip?
- **Card Three:** What can I be mindful of during this trip?
- **Card Four:** What is a significant outcome of this trip?
- **Card Five:** What is the primary purpose served by this trip?

It's good to bring your notes on the journey to compare what the cards offer with what happens.

We were planning a long trip to Greece in late 2019. While I am not a Hellenic Reconstructionist, the deities I most related to were Greek and the possibility of my making deeper connections to Them was strong. Several metaphorical roadblocks came up while we were putting the trip together. We ended up having a long conversation about whether we were getting signals from the universe that we shouldn't go. We decided to do a Tarot reading, asking, "Is traveling to Greece a good idea?" Looking back, that was a poorly worded question that reveals what we wanted the answer to be (some variation of, "yes, it is") The response was the Nine of Pentacles, the Hanged Man, and the Five of Cups (we used the Rider Waite deck). We looked at this and went, okay, this trip might be a little expensive, but it will give us a chance to rest and recuperate.

Nope. A ton of little things went wrong for us for the first half of the trip— accommodations were different from what we thought we were getting and we needed to be more in sync with cultural time references, weather-forced travel delays, and things like that. Nothing serious, but time and money-wasters, repeatedly. It all came to a head when my camera's memory card was, inexplicitly, wiped clean, and literally a thousand pictures disappeared the day I lost my passport. We should not have taken that trip, as the cards strongly indicated.

Journey-Specific Tarot Cards

Although any Tarot card, layout, and deck can offer insight, there are several cards everyone agrees are especially significant when it comes to travel.

- **The Fool:** Usually depicting a person walking along a mountain path, very close to the edge, if not about to walk right off the edge. The Fool is about new beginnings, exploring the unknown, and finding adventure. It can also warn of embarking without research and how those adventures are only sometimes fun, even when educational.

- **The Chariot:** Generally shown with two creatures pulling a vehicle under the guidance of someone, this is a card full of energy and confidence. The Chariot indicates longer journeys, often international in scope, and indicates one will easily overcome obstacles during that trip.
- **The Wheel of Fortune:** Here we see a vast wheel, often hanging without support in the sky. This is a tricky card because we always want it to indicate *good* fortune, but that is far from guaranteed. The Wheel offers insight into the nature of travel, of taking us to previously unknown places. It might be frightening and enlightening, but it will always bring change.
- **The Star:** This card often depicts a woman gracefully pouring liquid from a cup, sometimes accompanied by the presence of stars. Its symbolic essence embodies the concept of hope, inspiring a sense of optimism and possibility.
- **The Moon:** A Moon, a crescent curving inside the fullness, hangs in the center of the night sky, often with several creatures looking up at it. This card indicates that you need to allow your emotions and intuition to play a role in the journey. If this is a spiritual journey, this card is a potent indicator of unexpected issues and outcomes.
- **The Sun:** This card often shows a child riding a horse or other animal under a bright sun, neutral in expression. This joyful card brings a smile immediately, indicating that the plans will bring about an incredible journey.
- **The World:** While nothing usually shown on this card is travel-specific, it is very much so. Where it comes up in a layout will indicate what wisdom is available. Is the world yours for the asking? Or, instead, is the field too large? This is a card of *significant* opportunities and life-changing travels.
- **Aces:** All Aces represent new beginnings and offer insight into whether the journey ahead will bring you new things (pentacles), experiences (wands), emotions (cups), or perspectives (swords).
- **Knight of Pentacles:** Mounted on his horse, moving steadily along, this Knight indicates well-planned travels across well-

known areas (Think English countryside, rather than the Amazonian wilds). The Knight of Pentacles knows precisely where he is going and what he will do there.

- **Six of Swords**: A figure ferries a pair, one of whom is usually a child, across the water to a distantly seen shore. While this can feel like a somber card (swords are tricky that way), it indicates a journey by water, with others doing much of the work on your behalf. (Perhaps, a cruise?)
- **Two of Wands:** A wealthy figure stands on a stone balustrade holding a globe in hand. This person enjoys exploring the world as it brings wealth in many forms.
- **Three of Wands:** A figure stands on a high cliff watching ships depart. This is a card of fortune, of hopes relying on the triumphant return of the ships bringing riches and new things with them as the figure is in well-cut but patched clothes. It can indicate a journey by sea or the desire to expand one's horizons.
- **Eight of Wands:** Wands fly through the air, a lovely landscape shining below them. This card is specifically related to air travel, but always indicates swift travel—a great omen!
- **Knight of Wands:** Mounted on a horse, charging forward into the unknown, the Knight is riding into an adventure. With the land barren behind him, this card might specifically indicate desert or high mountain travel.
- **Eight of Cups**: A cloaked figure heads off into the unknown, leaving behind a carefully placed stack of cups. This is a card of adventure, seeking new places and leaving things to make homecoming pleasurable.

In general, any card that includes an object of travel—a boat, wheel, horse, path—or motion—walking, riding, swimming—indicates travel.

A Spell to Manifest Travel

Sometimes we want to take a trip to a specific place, but it looks impossible. You will need:

- Non-firing clay
- A lock of your hair and fingernails
- A pencil
- A paper map

Massage the hair and nails into the clay, then create a poppet of yourself using the top of the pencil as the core. Let the poppet cry thoroughly (you may choose to dress the poppet in a manner much like what you wear every day).

Use the poppet pencil to draw your journey from where you live to where you wish to go. Highways, airports, all the places along the way to where you want to go. This may take a long time, but the more energy you can place into the spell, the better it will work. You may wish to chant this charm or create one of your own:

"Over hills and through valleys, crossing rivers and seas, I will journey to (destination); it is my destiny."

When you go on this journey, take the poppet pencil with you, sharing the journey with it.

Simple Computer Magic

One thing that appeals to me about magic is how simple it can be to produce fantastic results. Changing my password to reflect my desire for a specific journey was a subtle energy shift that helped to manifest in a fantastic three-week journey through Italy. A variation on this would be to change your screensaver to images that inspire you, a favorite quotation, an affirmation, a beautiful mandala, or a nature scene. Use those moments when you turn your computer on to focus your energy on your desired outcome.

Practical Magic: Thoughts on What to Pack

Packing for a trip can be fun, but it feels like hard work for most people. People worry about forgetting something, looking weird and out of place compared to locals, or over-packing and hauling a big case around for no good reason. As you can see, I understand that, especially the over-packing problem. It took many travels for me to get over wanting to bring everything I might need. Here are my most valuable thoughts about packing, hard-won through the college of experience.

First, list activities you'll engage in on the journey, then what you'll need for each (remember shoes and accessories). Walking-around clothes, special occasion dinner outfit, getting sweaty because it's 40°C, falling in love with a beautiful stranger...all the different things you think are going to happen. At the same time, list extras you'll need: sunscreen, electrical adapters, and things specific to the trip. Hopefully, this will be fun; you'll be doing lots of daydreaming about the journey! Swimming in the Aegean Sea...hiking the trails on Mt. Rainier... sitting by the fire sipping cocoa in the Dolomites.... Spend all the time you need imagining the fun you'll have and what you'll need.

After years of dreaming, I was finally getting to Europe! Two weeks in Britain, mostly in London, but also a visit to Stratford-On-Avon by train, all shared with my eventually-going-to-be husband. We read many travel guides and made lists, then bought our first set of luggage—a pair of 35" rolling duffel bags. Looking back, I remember exactly why we thought we needed a carrying capacity of more than 130 liters, and we packed to the max: two pairs of sneakers, other walking shoes, sweaters, jeans, underwear, and socks for each day...we each filled our bags full and brought backpacks to boot!

Those bags were easily fifty pounds each and were a real pain (not just in the patootie) to manage on stairs, trains, and even when walking around. What saved us then (and the next couple of trips we used them for) was that our lodging was in a single place for a week or so at a time; we didn't need to deal much with packing, re-packing, and hauling.

At the start, this is a place to check whether you've got too much planned for the trip. Swimming and attending a fancy-dress ball is one kind of trip. If that same trip also includes hiking, sightseeing, and skiing, it's too much. You may feel like you need to cram it all in, but seeing lots of things quickly often feels more demanding (and more exhausting) than a smaller number of experiences deeply explored. This aligns with the more obviously magical things we discussed earlier. The less focus your trip has, the harder it will be for you to manifest the optimal experience. It's not impossible; you'll hear stories of people who do a little bit of everything on their journeys. Whether they pulled it off or not, it doesn't make it any less accurate that the lack of focus caused them to work much harder. Ask yourself, *what is it you want to accomplish on your trip?* If it's for relaxation, then exploring the nightlife of Tokyo is probably best saved for another trip. If you're traveling to the holy sites of Ireland to connect with your ancestors, ignore that your plane lands in Dublin—get your car and get gone. Or don't, and acknowledge that you'll be dividing your focus and energy between the ancestral sites and a night of pub crawls. Hey, pub crawls are fun! But the pubs will be there next time, and you told yourself that you had priorities.

Having compiled your initial list, look for ways to pare items down. In doing this, it's crucial to keep one rule in mind: no one will care if you wear the same clothes several days in a row.[21] Consider that two T-shirts worn over jeans can give you four days of clothes before you do laundry. Don't forget about clothes to wear to sleep in (a version of which I often wear on the flight) and accessories, like scarves. Will you want a purse or daypack (you rarely need both)?

Consider creating a capsule wardrobe. This collection of clothes all work together, usually within a neutral palette (I call them adult Garanimals; my base color is navy). A starting list for a capsule wardrobe might be two each of dresses, pants, and tops, with a sweater and jacket. If you have two similar items, choose the lightest weight. For instance, I never travel with my oversized, comfy, thick, cotton cable knit sweater, but instead take my thinner wool sweater. It's just as warm but takes up a quarter of the space. Plus, it's easier to layer on a coat if I need more warmth; at every step of packing, versatility is your ally.

One effective strategy to minimize the amount of luggage you carry is to incorporate regular laundry sessions into your travel plan, about once a week if possible. Many accommodations offer on-site washers, while hotels often provide laundry services, though be prepared for the usually steep costs associated with them. Researching local laundromats is also a viable option when needed. Personally, I've embraced this practice in every country I've visited, finding it to be an enlightening glimpse into the authentic local culture that most tourists yearn for. The time investment is modest, typically a couple of hours at most. While it may seem like a break from exploration, it grants you an opportunity to recharge. Furthermore, consider the trade-off between the time spent and the convenience of lighter, more manageable luggage. At the very least, washing essentials like

---

21 There may possibly be a single exception if you are going on a Very High-End trip, like traveling on the Orient Express from London to Istanbul or crossing the ocean on a luxury ship.

underwear and socks in the sink can suffice—just remember to allow them ample time to dry before reuse.

Lay out all the clothes you plan to travel with, then create outfits for all the events and activities you think you'll participate in. Look for ways to wear the same clothes in different combinations. If it helps, make it a game: how can you travel so that you wear every item at least twice during your trip? Plan to wear layers to keep warm rather than single bulky items. My raincoat has a hood and reaches my knees, making it perfect for everything but the worst inclement weather; even better, it has a zip-in lining, acting as a winter coat. This is the time to research the culture of your destination. Many city-based sacred sites have modesty provisions, like covering the head, upper arms, and legs to at least the knees. I've watched tourists in shorts—men and women both—turned away from a church in Rome. Make sure you know the condition of any sites you are visiting. You might be surprised to discover that an extraordinary place of magic and mystery is in the middle of an unmarked cow pasture. Reaching it may involve a modest walk through mud, knee-high brambles, or (if you're unlucky) both.

Create a comprehensive checklist of "extras" essential for your trip, such as sunscreen, medications, electrical adapters, and any specific necessities. It's highly likely that purchasing these items while traveling will come at a higher cost compared to bringing them from home. While everyone's habits differ, I often come across stories (even within my own household, ahem) of frantic last-minute searches for "the little things." The bags may be packed with clothes and accessories, yet these seemingly insignificant items that can make or break your journey are often left for the ambiguous "later."

Simple items brought from home create massive mood shifts: a picture of a dear one on the night table, an affirmation taped to the bathroom mirror, personal music playing...each encourages a sense of belonging and connection. Laying your scarves across a table or over a chair can transform an anonymous, generic room into a welcoming space.

One bit of magic is to create a common bond with your home, helping to ensure a safe return by preparing it for you to return. Do the dishes, give your home a basic clean, put away the laundry, clean the toilets, and remove the garbage. Bless the kitchen, the bedroom, the computer, the plants, and the altar. Returning home and feeling welcomed by the tidiness you left behind is a pleasure.

Non-clothing items that always come with me:

- **A hanging toiletries bag:** Like the compression packing cubes we started using about a decade ago, this has been a travel-ease changer. After every trip, no matter how short, I go through it and empty the contents, adding them to my daily rotation to be used up naturally. I refill the contents with brand new items when packing for the next trip (unless it's a very short interval between them), keeping toiletries fresh, nothing expired. Our version holds three silicone squeeze bottles and is wide enough for typical-sized toothbrushes to fit. There is a hook and a small, zippered mesh pouch at the top with two clear zippered areas below; the whole kit folds and zippers closed into a compact bag smaller than a pair of shoes.

Other than basic toiletries (like shampoo, toothpaste, and deodorant), the specific items I always carry in this bag are:

- **Tweezers:** From plucking hair to fishing out small items from tight places, tweezers are essential. You can even use them as a makeshift screwdriver.
- **Dental floss:** If you carry the unflavored variety, you've got a string to tie things together, measure things, and even cut cheese. Not to mention its actual purpose of being able to get those super annoying pieces of food out from between your teeth.
- **Petroleum jelly:** A small tube of this stuff offers a quick balm for super dry skin, but it also makes squeaky hinges silent.

Additional items I always pack are:

- **Cloth bag for laundry:** Mine is cotton with a drawstring and came from a long-ago hotel. I like having a specific place to keep dirty laundry (especially the stinky items) so they don't go into "gen pop." Sometimes the bag goes into a single piece of luggage as we combine all the clean things into the other bag; when we get to a place with a washer, it's all in one place, and easier to toss it all to be cleaned.

- **Two-gallon sealable bag:** If there is any possibility of water events on your trip, this is easy to include. But it's also helpful to keep an item utterly separate from other clothes, like that bottle of perfume you bought. There are few things worse than liquids leaking in your luggage, and having a sealable bag adds a layer of security.
- **A quart-size clear sealable bag:** This is the bag for any liquid add-ons you need for your journey: sunscreen, bug spray, etc.—anything that you might need to show TSA or other security authorities. If you aren't checking your toiletry bag, you'll put liquids into this bag to go through security.
- **Shopping bag:** My bag folds smaller than a pack of cards. Many places outside the United States charge for shopping bags; some don't even offer them to shoppers. Having your own helps you fit in better with the locals and show respect for the environment. It can also double as another carry-on bag if you need it.
- **Compression packing cubes:** These have made an enormous difference in my travel experience. Using them, I can use a smaller piece of luggage to carry as much as I brought before. My non-scientific testing tells me that I can pack as much as 30% more when using these cubes. Note that I use compression cubes, not just packing cubes. The latter is great for organizing your clothes, but not for bringing much more.
- **Stainless steel cutlery:** Several years ago, I started carrying a stainless-steel spork and straw with me. Environmentally speaking, it makes a minimal difference, but it's been helpful on several occasions.
- **Detergent strips:** The biggest secret to traveling light relies on being able to do laundry regularly. Using these strips, which travel in a sealable bag that can be repurposed if needed, does away with all the downsides of liquid detergent. They add essentially no weight and can be torn into smaller pieces to use in smaller spaces (like hotel sinks or tubs).

The "always with me and never in a checked bag" list is even more specific: my medication, wallet, travel case, jewelry case, a change of underwear, all electronics (typically, my camera, e-reader, and laptop) and their cables, power adapter, pen, journal, stainless steel water bottle, and a small bag that holds tissues, eye drops, moisturizer, aspirin, hair clip, and a comb. My travel valet is slightly bigger than a wallet and holds my passport, credit card, identity card, and cash. There is a place for a SIM card and a clasp to hold it closed. My jewelry case is just a tiny drawstring bag to hold the little bit I travel with—I never take any precious jewelry when I travel, not so much from a fear of being robbed but because it's too easy to lose an earring or have a piece broken. I always carry a bag of tea with throat-soothing or sleep-inducing properties; hot water is easy to get almost anywhere.

Items that are often included in my travels:

- **Luggage scale:** If traveling in Europe, consider carrying a handheld luggage scale. It doesn't take up much space and can save you a ton of money. Outside the United States, many travel operators have strict rules about luggage size and weight. Your rolling carry-on, for example, might be perfectly sized but over the maximum weight—and the carriers who are most likely to check have stiff fees ($85 at a recent look) for being overweight.
- **Deck of cards and cribbage board:** My family played cribbage on camping trips and travels throughout my childhood, and I almost always carry a deck and small folding board with me. Of course, the board isn't necessary; you can get by with just pen and paper to keep track of the score.
- **Mini umbrella:** Purchased because of a downpour at a National Trust site years ago, my umbrella has been a mainstay for years.
- **Hand fan:** Menopause was no fun, and I carried a hand fan with me everywhere I went, and its usefulness remains during every visit to a hot weather environment.

Other items you might want:

- Portable charger
- Collapsible water bottle
- Hat
- Compression sock
- Passport case
- Cross-body bag
- Cable organizer
- Shoe bags
- Extra memory cards for your camera
- Eye mask
- Earplugs
- Quick-dry microfiber towel

Chapter Four

Tools for the Journey

We've thought about where we're going and made the necessary reservations. We have prepared what we are taking with intention and thoughtful consideration of our options. We've also reviewed the fundamentals of magic and how to get our correspondences aligned with our plans and preferences. All of this has created a powerful and versatile set of tools to make our travels safer and more adventurous. In this chapter, we will use our tools and bring our focused will and magic to bear to facilitate our desire to travel, protect ourselves while traveling, and get ourselves home safely when all is said and done.

As I've said before, once you've digested everything here, you should look at this chapter as a reference guide to be sifted through for what is most valuable to you, depending on the occasion. Doing everything I'm about to describe would be a tremendous (and likely overwhelming) amount of work, and it wouldn't apply uniformly to what you have planned! Sort out what makes sense for the trip you are planning, make your preparations, and then do the work so you can have the most rewarding travel experience possible!

Working With Sigils

Using specifically chosen or designed symbols in magical practice is some of the oldest magic we know, dating from the earliest peoples of the Neolithic era. We can see their symbolic art in the cave paintings of Europe and the unbroken fifty-thousand-year line of use within the Aboriginals tribes in Australia. The term sigil itself comes from the Latin *sigillum*, meaning "seal." There are references to seals being used to bind or summon supernatural forces going back to Babylonian,

Sumerian, and Egyptian cultures. For the magical traveler, sigils offer a quick and straightforward method to work your magic.

Sigils are symbols you imbue with magic, making them a kind of spell. All symbols—*kanji,* letters, runes, etc.—can be sigils if you imbue them with magical energy. For our purpose, however, sigils are symbols you intentionally create; doing so makes them personal. When creating them, you keep your goal in mind, infusing the entire process with your magical intent. Don't be dissuaded by performance anxiety about your artistic skills! Whether you've got serious design skills or can't draw a straight line unaided, it *does not matter.* Sigils represent something to you alone; at most, you can expand them to those you travel with. They aren't going up in a gallery somewhere, and they aren't going online (unless you put them there).

Do this for me: try them. I have countless stories of students who resisted working with sigils or similar arts-and-crafts-related projects, only to treasure the results when they were finished. Can I guarantee you'll love them? No. You might try the methods outlined below and hate the results. That's fine; now you know and can move on to other options. I know there's no guarantee that you will know what you think about these until you try them!

Here are several methods for creating a sigil, all based on wanting to have a safe journey by airplane.

Method One: Images

Think about an airplane (you may want to look at a picture). On a piece of paper, draw a small plane with a smile (however, other imagery may feel correct to you). Overlap the smile on the plan and see what shape emerges from the overlapping areas. This method is best for people who have strong positive artistic skills.[22]

---

22 I don't. But I am happy to print out an image and trace over it.

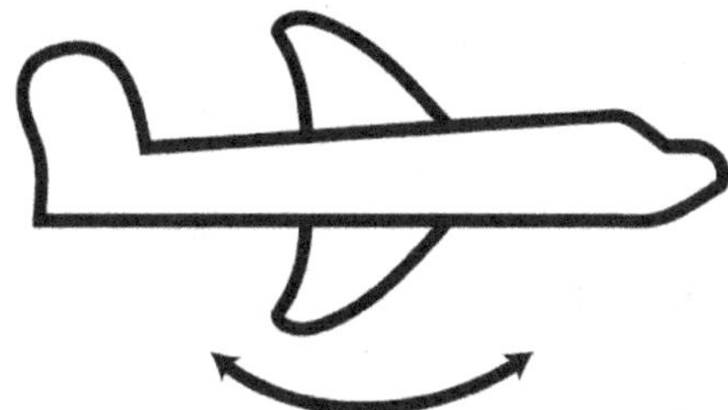

Smile Plane Image Sigil

Method Two: Written Affirmation

Affirmations are concisely worded positive statements that you use to manifest the outcomes you want. They should always be phrased in the present tense—you don't want to be healthy (or whatever your goal is) "someday," you want it to be in your life now. You might choose the affirmation for a safe plane trip: "*I fly safely from start to finish.*" Write that phrase on paper as one word in all caps: IFLYSAFELY-FROMSTARTTOFINISH. Remove any letters that duplicate, thus creating "IFLYSAEROMTNH." Use those letters—upright, upside down, sideways, or backward—to create a unique sigil. See the image below for an example I created.

Phrase as Sigil

I suggest using the symbol of your affirmation as a support, rather than a replacement, for repeating the phrase to yourself. Having it marked on a notebook, your luggage, or anything within your view will prompt you to recall your affirmation and use it. Reinforcing your will with this symbol will only be for the good.

Method Three: Magic Square

A square containing numbers is considered magical when the numbers total the same amount when added in all directions, horizontally, vertically, and diagonally. For example, the square in the Lo Shu Grid example totals fifteen in each direction. There are a variety of magic squares one can use. The earliest is the Lo Shu Grid (or *Luohu* square), found in a text about mathematics called *Shushu Jiyi* (or, *Memoir on Some Traditions of Mathematical Art*), said to be written in 190 BCE. Most other squares are larger than 3x3, making them useless for sigil work. But, in the fourteenth century, the mathematician Narayana Pandit created a new magic square (a variation of the Lo Shu grid), declaring that the study of magic squares constructs yantra, thereby destroying the ego of bad mathematicians and for the pleasure of good mathematicians (see table below). Whether this grid will destroy your ego is a question I leave for the reader to resolve, but it can benefit our purposes. Finally, in the tenth century, Islamic scholars devised a new variation, the Rasa'il grid.

4	9	2
3	5	7
8	1	6

Lo Shu Grid

8	1	6
3	5	7
4	9	2

Narayana Grid

2	7	6
9	5	1
4	3	8

Rasa'il Grid

Magic Square Grid Variations

To use a magic square to create a sigil, choose which grid to use. If you feel you've got some personal attachment to any of them via a shared culture, great. Otherwise, let your intuition be your guide. Then create your affirmation (we'll use the one from above, "I fly safely"). Translate the letters into numbers using this standard alphabet conversion chart, then eliminate consecutive numbers.

1	2	3	4	5	6	7	8	9
A	B	C	D	E	F	G	H	I
J	K	L	M	N	O	P	Q	R
S	T	U	V	W	X	Y	Z	

Alphabet to Number Conversion Chart

Our phrase becomes 9 637 116537; removing the duplicate numbers leaves us with 963716537.

Insert a circle into the first and last number in your grid. Then draw a line connecting each number in consecutive order to create your unique sigil. Unlike some other methods in this section, the result will be simultaneously more abstract and a direct artistic representation. Still, to the informed viewer (e.g., you), it will be more directly derived from the underlying mantra.

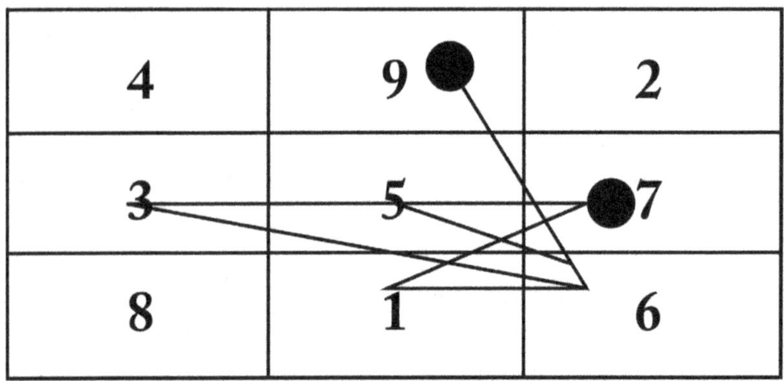

Alpha-Numeric Sigil Using Lo Shu Grid

The final sigil looks like this:

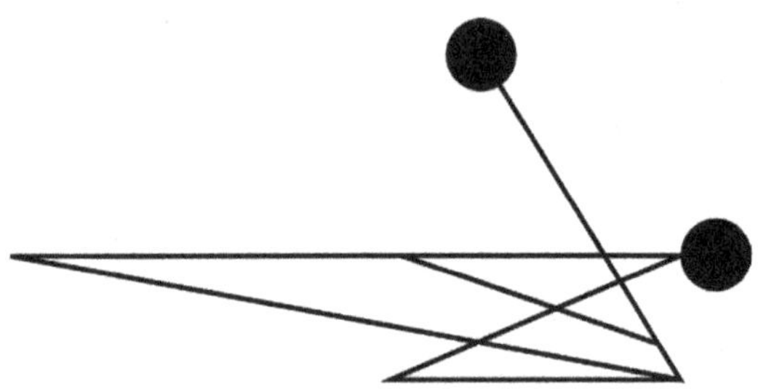

Method Four: Using Personal Symbols

This is the most time-intensive method based on the work of Laura Tempest Zakroff, expanding on the universal experience of developing a collection of symbols for our use, like a heart for love or XXXs and

OOOs to signify kisses and hugs (I have my unique take on the classic smiley face that is instantly recognizable to the few who have seen it. That may sound basic, but my husband assures me he could pick mine out of a line-up of hundreds). Between your unique symbols and your personal take on common ones (like my smiley!), you likely have already developed an arsenal of personalized glyphs. Developing custom, purpose-built symbols is simply an extension of this logic, although by starting from scratch, you'll have some work waiting for you.

For example, let us consider a protective symbol for air travel. Based on our example of flying safely, we would brainstorm solutions—what does that mean to us? Some answers might be taking off and landing safely, having a smooth flight, or sleeping through the flight. In general, choose positive outcomes to represent rather than trying to enforce "not happens" (i.e., no bumps, no turbulence). The negative/canceling actions are always more challenging to translate into concrete magical language, particularly into a concise visual short of using the ubiquitous circle-and-line.

We would then look at the keywords (perhaps "land," "safely," "smooth," and "sleep") and draw out whatever marks might resonate for us for each. I might draw a swoop representing the plane taking off or landing safely, a straight line for smoothness, and ZZZs for sleep. Combine those symbols into a shape that pleases.

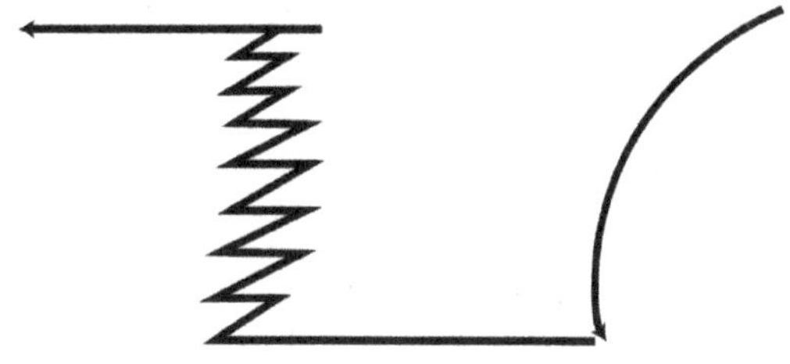

Personal Symbol

In my case, I would make multiple versions to choose the one that most appeals to me. A more intuitive thinker might feel that their first draft is typically their best and will go no further. Use your best practice from other parts of your life. Once you have arrived at the symbol you will use, you are ready to activate it.

Redraw the sigil on a clean piece of paper, imbuing the image with the power and strength of your intent (that way, you'll have a copy of what you initially chose so you can use it again or add it to your journal). Find as quiet a spot as you can and calm your mind (this is where having that regular meditation practice can help. I recognize, however, that you may not be able to control your surroundings, so do your best. Even if it's just taking three deep breaths and focusing on each part of that process, you will bring greater calm to the moment). Hold the paper in both hands and feel the energy flow out of you into the paper as you consider the sigil's meaning and importance to you. Keep looking until you realize your vision has become a little blurry, then destroy the sigil.

If you have privacy, burning the paper is ideal. You can also:

- Tear the paper into pieces.
- Soak it in water until it's just a soggy lump and the ink has washed away, then flush it down the toilet.[23]
- Bury the paper in the earth.
- Release it into the air.

If you have no privacy and are indoors, blow on the sigil and concentrate on the power dissipating to do your will. Do not look at the sigil after that but crumple it and recycle the paper.

The final piece is to put the sigil and its task out of your mind. Metaphorically you want to walk away from it, knowing it will work. The more you think about your sigil, the more difficult it'll be to carry on with your life. Take a moment to appreciate that you have manifested the energy you want to see in your life, and let the universe decide what happens next.

Permanent Sigil Options

Sigils are versatile and can be incorporated into permanent places to provide long-term or constant magic (protective sigils are particularly good at this). Consider making your name into a sigil infused with

23 If, and only if, your piece of paper is *very* tiny.

the intent that anything the sigil inscribed onto remains yours forever. Doing so creates a spell of protection against loss or theft.

Other ideas:

- Draw the sigil using special ink on handmade paper; frame it and hang it in a place that is always visible.
- Save a picture and make it your phone or computer background.
- Cross-stitch or embroider your sigil into curtains, rugs, or bed linens. Alternatively, use the sigil-marked cloth to create a spell bag, as clothing, or carry it with you. I often bring a pillowcase from home to sleep on, and a tiny sigil is embroidered into one corner to bring me excellent sleep.
- Draw on rocks placed around your home. When traveling, draw with water infused with herbs whose energy aligns with your intent or the ash from burning your sigil. Rain will wash the rock clean eventually (do not use salt water, as it can damage surfaces).
- Add to fresh-poured concrete, under flooring, or into walls (we did this with one of our former homes).
- Paint on walls before painting over with the same color.
- Draw one on an amulet to wear or attach to a piece of luggage.
- Inscribe a sigil into a piece of clay, glaze, then fire. If small enough, you can drill a hole into one end before glazing and firing; wear it as an amulet.

Some options are semi-permanent, at best:

- Draw a sigil onto a candle as part of a spell.
- Place a printed image behind your phone in its case.
- Stir into your tea or coffee.
- Draw on the fogged mirror after a shower.
- Tuck it into your wallet.
- Draw on your body with a pen. You could make this permanent with tattooing but be very sure of the design before doing so.
- Create out of food and consume. This is particularly fun with pancake batter.

- Draw on money and tuck it into a wallet (spend or not, each creates and fulfills different intentions)

Magical Everyday Items

I love the people in our community who wear their life boldly. Their clothes, jewelry, and tattoos proudly proclaim their spiritual orientation. I am not one of them, preferring to navigate life in the background, rarely putting myself "out there." Even so, I still carry magical talismans and sigils with me; they are just less noticeable, and mostly, I use my jewelry.

Magic Jewelry

Earrings whisper wisdom into my ears, amplifying my intuition with every sway. Necklaces serve as guardians, nurturing the energy centers of my throat, heart, or solar plexus, their chain lengths attuned to their purpose. Rings hold a special place in my heart, as they unite with elemental energies, each one a symbol of connection and power.

Before I do anything specific with my jewelry, I magically cleanse and reset its energy. To do so, I create sacred space, then add three pinches of sea or kosher salt to a bowl of clean water. Iodized salt should be avoided if possible; "impurity" might be strong language for a nutritional supplement, but it still represents a dilution of the salt itself for our purpose. I stir the water with my finger nine times to dissolve the salt, then submerge the jewelry.

While submerged, I say:

"Blessings to you, beautiful jewelry
Release all negativity
By Earth, Air, Fire, and Sea
As I will, so mote it be!"

Then I dry the piece thoroughly with a cotton cloth. If I intend to use it soon, I'll wear it for days; otherwise, it is carefully placed in my jewelry box, a clean slate for subsequent use.

There are caveats to this work that you should remember: not all materials can be submerged in salted water. Some stones dissolve in water or are damaged by salt, including turquoise, hematite, fluorite, opal, labradorite, and pyrite. Be mindful and choose an alternate cleaning process, such as this one:

Physically wash the item by rubbing it with a soft cloth and using a soft bristle brush. Place the item on cotton cloth in bright sunlight for at least nine minutes and as much as an hour. While in the sunlight, before it's finished cleansing, speak the same charm I shared above, which I use for cleansing my jewelry.

These cleansings can be used for any item you use as a charm.

Just as a crystal can be infused with intention and energy, we have the power to imbue everyday objects with an extra layer of protection and strength. Whether it's through jewelry, keychains, hair accessories, shoelaces, socks, underwear, purses, or wallets, anything that can be carried on our person becomes a vessel for our magical intentions.

Here are some examples I've used:

- An eloquence charm placed on a stone tucked into a pocket before going into a high-level meeting to convince higher-ups to change a policy they wanted to implement.
- A keychain imbued with "safe travel" energy.
- A charm made from a piece of metal engraved for soothing energy, worn before family gatherings.

When we infuse everyday objects with our intentions—thereby turning them into charms—we become active participants in co-creating a magical universe. By doing so, we enhance our manifestation abilities and carry that empowering energy with us at all times, reminding ourselves of our agency in living our best lives. Keeping magic confined to specific times and places diminishes its power, but embracing it on our journeys signifies that magical thinking has a place everywhere and at all times.

These wearable charms can be energized in the moment, created for specific purposes, or worn all the time. Each is activated with a specific, two-phrase sentence and works until the energy runs out. Recharging is usually done by giving the item a rest, letting it charge up in the light of the Sun or Moon, or actively filling it with your energy. Activating phrases are like affirmations: keep the phrase short, focused, and positive. One phrase describes the item, the other its purpose. For example, my safe travel keychain has a wire cage into which various stones can be placed (I love its versatility!). Before our ferry crossed the Aegean Sea, I put a piece of aquamarine into the cage and held it in my right (dominant) hand. I ensured its energy was "topped up" and said, "With this keychain, my travels are calm; I am safe from harm."

Other energizing statement examples might include:

- "These shoelaces keep me focused and calm. Wearing them, I am grounded and centered."
- "This bracelet connects me to the loving compassion of Tara. Wearing it helps me take nothing personally."
- "This belt activates the energy of my creativity. I am a creature with an unlimited imagination."
- "These undies are nearly as sexy as I am; when my lover sees them, they will want more of what I offer."

No matter the situation, it is possible for the items that you wear or keep about you to magically align with your intentions. It thus follows that when you expect to be traveling, it is ideal for those things you have already chosen with intention and forethought to be further aligned with your purposes by letting them be the bearer of these charms.

Enchanting Clothing

Harnessing the power of magic in your everyday life can be as simple as infusing your ordinary clothes with enchantments. This remarkable practice allows you to carry your spells and intentions discreetly, without attracting undue attention, except perhaps on a nude beach. The best part? The process involves just two steps.

First, cleanse the garment using an environmentally responsible method of your choosing. It is recommended to perform this cleansing yourself, as it helps remove any residual energy left behind by previous handlers. Even if you've owned the garment for ages, it's still essential to cleanse it, preparing it to become a potent magical item.

Whether using a machine or your sink, use cold water and add some sea or kosher salt. Iodized salt is not ideal because it is not pure, so you'll get off on the wrong foot from the outset. You do not need to use detergent unless the item is secondhand or previously worn—because who wants someone else's funk on their clothes? Ick!

If it cannot be water-cleaned (I'm particularly thinking about silk and other delicate materials like velvet), then you'll have to energetically cleanse it another way after getting the "normal" cleaning done as you always would. Waving it through sandalwood incense is excellent for small items. Larger pieces or those with much energetic gunk in them do best by being turned inside out and hung in sunlight for several hours. If you are concerned about sun damage, hang the item in the moonlight for three nights. You'll know the garment is energetically clean because it will feel lighter.

After the garment has been cleaned, charge it with your intention. Hold it so you can run your hands all over it; you want to cover it entirely with your energetic intent. Contemplate what your intent is for this garment. Protection from unkind gaze? The ability to speed through transit centers? Clear thinking? Decide what you want, then spend a few minutes centering yourself, gathering your energy, and taking three deep breaths. When you feel ready, push energy through your hands as you slowly run your hand over the garment. Feel the energy seep into the fabric's weave, becoming part of it. If you have a specific intent or scenario, describe the best possible outcome while energizing the item.

If you sew, consider sewing a sigil onto the label of your clothing or on a piece of unique fabric to tuck into your wallet or purse. Before my husband hiked the length of Hadrian's Wall, I sewed sigils for endurance into his socks (I also wrote tiny sigils for his health on his water bottle and clear communication on a piece of paper I slipped into his phone case).

Consider a few things we consistently have with us when we leave the house: keys, wallet, phone, and clothes. Those clothes you wear change daily, but your shoes may not. There is a ton of folklore about shoes, steps, and turns of phrase. Why not use them as inspiration and draw the sigils you need on your shoes? A bit of chalk or pencil will work perfectly.

In Your Room

Since my first international trip, I've carried a set of ritual tools with me when I travel. It looks like a mini sewing kit tucked into an embroidered box I picked up in Chinatown when I was a teen. A popular mint's tin container makes an unobtrusive kit, and I've seen plain versions in craft stores that can be decorated as you desire. A film canister (am I dating myself?) makes an excellent tiny altar kit. Another version (that I talked about in *A Witch's Guide to Crafting Your Practice*) uses a drawstring bag that doubles as an altar cloth. Stitch a ½-inch hem around the edge of your chosen cloth, run a cord through it, then knot it at the ends. When you pull the cord tight, it creates a drawstring bag.

My kit always has a birthday candle (the smallest candles I can easily find), penny, needle, thimble, and thread in several colors; I sometimes add specific stones or a small vial of blended oil if I know in advance that I'll be doing a particular ritual (such as celebrating a sabbat) while traveling. I can usually get matches or a lighter wherever I am, so I rarely bring them, although the kit would be more complete if I included them. It's my habit to stick a few blank sticky notes into my travel journal, so I almost always have a piece of paper to write on for petitions or sigils, but I've used pages torn from that journal in an emergency.

Each item represents an element and links to my usual ritual tools:

- **Birthday candle:** Fire, wand
- **Penny:** Earth, pentacle
- **Needle:** Air, athame
- **Thimble:** Water, chalice

I use the thread to wrap my petitions as a substitute for burning them, an infrequent option (smoke alarms are not conducive to ritual work!). If I can bring an essential oil, my first choice is a blend I make of peppermint and sweet orange, which brings mental clarity, reduced anxiety, and generally brightens one's mood. Most people like lavender, which is often very easy to find, but it's a scent I do not like, so it'll never be on my list. If you like it, lavender calms anxiety and promotes sleep. Other options might include tea tree (cleansing), lemon (mental clarity and improved mood), and clary sage (stress relief).

When using essential oils, *always* mix them into a neutral carrier oil, like grapeseed or almond oil. Essential oils are potent and can quickly burn skin or create a rash over time, even if the oil didn't cause a reaction the first time you tried it. I recommend that you use no more than two drops of essential oil for a five-milliliter vial (about one teaspoon of combined oil). Since the quantities are so tiny, bringing a variety of premixed oils with you is easy. Consider bringing oil blends for headache relief, honoring a sabbat, keeping negativity at bay, or as a tribute to a specific deity.

Crystal quartz is undeniably my go-to stone when it comes to my magical practices. Its versatility is unparalleled, allowing it to be easily programmed with intentions, energies, or desired outcomes. However, when I have a specific type of magic in mind, I make it a point to bring along a stone that complements and amplifies that particular working. Among the most frequently found stones in my ritual kit, alongside quartz, are amethyst, carnelian, coral, and turquoise. These gemstones each possess their own unique properties and vibrational energies, lending a powerful boost to my magical endeavors.

Chapter Five

Companions for the Journey

A dear friend of mine has an administrative job with the United States Department of State and is an excellent source for stories of world travel. Every few years, they go somewhere new in the world, often an out-of-the-way place you wouldn't usually think of as a "destination." In Japan (I did say "usually"), they learned that before travelers leave, they often acquire a small green frog plush toy to bring them safety.[24] Where I live in Portugal, the Catholic way of life is very strong culturally, even if not so much spiritually. Here, people are more likely to carry a silver St. Christopher medallion to stay safe while traveling. In both cases, the aim is to invoke divine protection for the traveler, echoing similar practices carried out across many different faiths over the centuries.

The desire for these charms is natural. It's comforting to think that we have a guardian while we travel, a being more far-seeing than ourselves to act as a lookout and protector for us, giving ourselves more protection when we venture beyond the safe boundaries of our everyday life. Likewise, our loved ones may worry about our well-being while traveling and offer up prayers (another kind of magic) or charms to do what they can. A lit candle in a window is an Irish tradition going back to the 1600s; it has many different meanings depending on whom you ask, but a common belief is that it is a boon to travelers, sometimes promising a place to rest for those in need, sometimes simply a sign of well-wishing.

---

24 Apparently, this tradition comes from a pun. *Buji* means "safe" and kaeru means both "frog" and "return"; a *bujikaeru* is therefore a "safe (frog) journey." (L. G., personal communications, October 27, 2022)

For several years after college, I lived in New York City. It was just before Mayor Rudy Giuliani's infamous civic cleanup, and parts of the city—many central—were actively dangerous. Bryant Park (now the site of the glamourous bi-annual Fashion Week) was essentially an open-air drug market. Grand Central Terminal's gorgeous beaux-arts glory was hidden behind the filth from its daily usage as a flophouse. The Port Authority Bus Terminal offered arriving travelers the dubious opportunity to dodge beggars, drunks, and thieves. It was beyond gritty; it was gross. One of the results of this environment is that, during my time there, I was thrown into the deep end of self-preservation. Over time, I perfected my bubble of protection. Made up of pure energy, it combined "keep away" with a bit of "nothing to see here" and allowed me to travel around the city safely and unmolested.

Bubble of Protection

Initially, creating this bubble will take time, so practice in places of safety to get the hang of it. As you grow more comfortable with the process, you will get faster. I used it so often that it usually only took me a few seconds to be enclosed entirely within the bubble.

- To begin, feel your connection to the earth. Feel that energy connecting within you.
- Feel your breath as you calmly breathe normally and easily. Feel the energy of the air connecting with your own.
- Draw upon the Earth and Air energy guided by the power within you and feel it fill your body. You should feel a bit "stuffed," maybe a little buzzy from the extra energy.
- When you can't add any more energy into yourself, push the energy out of you in an oval all around you, including your feet (causing it to project into the ground a little bit; that's fine).

You may wish to think of this energy as having a color, like gold, that feels protective. The energy should be equally thick and dense all around you and doesn't need to extend for more than a few inches. Some people imagine a *Star Trek* transporter effect or a more soap bubble flowy look; use whatever imagery feels protective to you. What's important is that you have a visualization in mind that comes easily to you. Otherwise, you're putting a speed bump on the path to your bubble. Snapping the image into place immediately will be more efficient for you in the long run. It will also help you maintain the bubble throughout a tense or anxious situation. KISS: Keep It Simple, Silly.

As you push the energy out, know what it is intended to do and add that intention into the energy itself, like a silver thread woven into a piece of fabric. You should see the thread as though it was always there, a fundamental part of the bubble's structure. This intention can be whatever you need. You might start with "don't bother me" or "ill intent can't see me." Specificity is always reasonable, but if you get too specific (e.g., "drive away pickpockets"), you've just left yourself open to every other kind of trouble. My examples above are an excellent place to start.

"Tie" the bubble off when it is the size you want it to be by visualizing it staying at the size and energy it is—like you do with a balloon. Then link a tiny bit of your energy into the shield from your solar plexus to keep it powered. If the balloon imagery is working for you, picture it as a string tied to it. I've heard geekier Witches describe the tether as you might see on a space suit during a "walk." It can be as simple as a small tendril leading from you to the bubble's surface.

The bubble of protection isn't infinite, and you will want to consciously pull the energy back into yourself, or you will grow tired trying to maintain it all the time. Try to prioritize what locations you'll be in; you are probably overtaxing yourself if you're keeping your bubble up while in your hotel room. Also, this isn't *Star Trek,* even if you visualize it like that—you don't have an actual force field. I know it sounds obvious, but there's a difference between shedding the attention of trouble and dealing with it if it latches on to you. Participate in your protection to enhance your bubble. Act the part.

Calling the Guardians

In many alternative spiritualities, there is a long history of working with the four quarters representing the four classical elements (Earth, Air, Fire, and Water) when we perform spells and rituals. These personifications of the elements have also been called Watchtowers, which hearkens to their ancient duty as powerful observers guarding the material plane against evil from other realms. Calling upon these beings is a good choice if you feel threatened and have time to do a longer warding.

This entire exercise presumes you are doing it in your mind for privacy. In the physical realm, you may sit quietly with your eyes closed, palms up, and open in your lap. It may be difficult, but try to get yourself to a neutral state with steady breathing and a calm, loose demeanor.

To begin, face East, towards the direction of the rising sun. Hold your arms up, elbows at your waist, and hands open welcomingly. Looking up, slightly above the horizon, call out:

"Guardians of the East, hear my plea
I need your inspiration; protect me!
As I will, so mote it be!"

Wait until you feel the East Guardian; perhaps it has words for you? It may not, but it's polite to wait with the possibility of also gaining free guidance. The Guardian isn't going to leave now, so once it finishes, or if it never speaks (which is fine), move on.

You'll then face South, towards the direction of the noonday sun. Yes, this is a little awkward if you're sitting on the floor. But you're not trying to impress anyone and are probably alone anyway. In a pinch, it won't ruin your work if you can't move about (to avoid drawing attention, for example), but as I've often said, it's a speed bump on your path. Hold your arms up, elbows at your waist, and hands open welcomingly. Looking directly overhead, call out:

"Guardians of the South, hear my plea
I need your energy; protect me!
As I will, so mote it be!"

Again, wait until you feel the South Guardian; perhaps it has words for you? Whether it speaks to you or not, acknowledge its presence, and continue the ritual.

Now, face West, towards the direction of the setting sun. Hold your arms up, elbows at your waist, and hands open welcomingly. Looking out, slightly below the horizon, call out:

"Guardians of the West, hear my plea
I need your wisdom; protect me!
As I will, so mote it be!"

Wait now until you feel the West Guardian; as before, offer your time to them should they want it. Greet them as you have the others; don't shortcut any of these things because you're repeating them! That's not usually a problem, but speed bumps, right?

Finally, face North, towards the direction of the midnight sun. Hold your arms up, elbows at your waist, and hands open welcomingly. Looking down, call out:

"Guardians of the North, hear my plea
I need your strength; protect me!
As I will, so mote it be!"

Wait until you feel the North Guardian; allow it to converse with you as before. Acknowledge this guardian and then expand your focus to take all four in.

Having invited the Guardians, speak with them directly and describe your need. Be thorough; they aren't in any hurry. Tell as much of a story as you need to give the entire situation and think through what help you want. This could be watching over you or a more substantial push away than your bubble generates; there are as many options as their situations. Heed their wisdom and direction. When you are finished, thank them each in turn:

"Guardian of [direction], you were well-come.
Go if you must, stay if you will.
Farewell, and blessed be!"

As usual, ensure you ground your energy when you are done, and if time permits, reflect further on your interaction with the Guardians. My experience with them has never been particularly cryptic, but every entity in my sphere knows I don't understand subtlety very well—hit me over the head, or don't bother telling me! But that's me and my world; there's no reason to think this is universally true.

Working With Deities

Before we look at working with a deity, let me emphasize that there is no need to work with a name to do travel (or any) magic. Called *immanent deity* by Starhawk and *non-theistic Paganism* in more recent literature, this model for energy offers a path to power that does not rely on an external (also called *transcendent*) force to make our magic work. It does mean that you may rely on something other than having a definite name to call upon during your workings. Still, some (my husband is one) are otherwise perfectly fine with supernatural concepts, but have never had an ecstatic experience (in some cases, they rejected an awareness of what I would call a "deity" for their own [good and excellent] reasons). This may sound like a "speed bump" situation to some of you, especially if you don't relate to it, but look back on the sections relating to the surety of intent. Calling out to Ra (for example) if you don't think that there is such a being sets up a false dynamic, and you'll know it as you do it. If you do that, you've undermined yourself from the outset.

On the other hand, if you have a non-theistic view, calling upon deities is not forbidden. Instead, allow yourself the notion that you are naming an aspect of the energy you are calling upon. In other words, if you want to do a spell for wisdom and insight, there's no harm in framing that aspect of the world's power as Athena if only to make visualization easier. Saying, "Athena, guide my hand," is more efficient than saying, "universal forces of nature and the group mind that sees all, guide my hand"; if you are using that name similarly to the correspondences I wrote about in Chapter Two, then it's doubly robust. Of course, none of this is necessary for you if you don't have any difficulty grasping completely abstract forces in your mind. This is one of the more complicated yet reassuring aspects of alternative spirituality: that the power of divinity is found within us all and yet is not the same for us all.

Many of us outside of mainstream religion are polytheistic, which means we believe in the existence of multiple deities, beings who come to us from many cultures and pantheons. When we choose to work with a deity, we often look first to our heritage (in my case, Celtic and Central European), by need (such as working with White Tara to develop compassion), or even because They chose us. My principal deities are both Roman, and many are the story of Pagans describing signs they were receiving from a deity native to cultures thousands of miles away. Bottom line: your relationship with a deity is something only you can come to.

In some ways, a relationship with a deity is like any relationship: there's a beginning, middle, and perhaps even an end. There's an introduction of some kind; either you are seeking them or them seeking you, or perhaps pure serendipity (although I don't trust that much when it comes to deity). Exploration occurs, wherein you'll learn more about their likes and dislikes and whether compatibility exists. If it isn't, respectfully say, "thank you, but no." I don't recommend ghosting a god! Remember (for the moment, presuming you are on "Team Deity") that these beings are eternal and infinite.[25] However, if there does seem to be a connection, a proper relationship will begin to take shape.

What a relationship looks like can resemble the other relationships in your life: parents, friends, lovers, acquaintances, etc. All these are entirely plausible relationships with deity, although not every model

25 For one thing, they are definitely seeing other people.

may fit your situation. Some insist that a deity chooses you. Others (including myself, way back in the day) choose the relationship based on need or desire. Some people's relationships with deities began with the deity reaching out in the practitioner's dreams or rituals, and sometimes they couldn't identify who it was and had to research.

So why does this matter? We should be aimed at how these deities can participate in our traveling magic, right? We are. When you call upon these deities for your magic, the nature of your relationship with them is critical. As an example, what if you needed to borrow a moderately substantial amount of money? How you would ask your parents is wildly different from asking a lover or your friends, right?

In the same way, if the message you convey to deity is, "would you please help me out? I'm traveling to Suriname. I've never been and am a little scared, but I want to do it" (from the perspective of a parental figure), you'd be coming to them as their child looking for comfort. On the other hand, a lover would likely be more straightforward—you've got a level of intimacy that allows you to get to the heart of things immediately. They'll tell you that you can handle things, you are great at XYZ, and that will see you through. If you brought that same message to friends, you would likely get practical help; restaurants to go to that you can trust, maybe a reliable tour guide. Deciding which deity to work with is roughly similar. Do you want Dionysus to power a charm to guide you in your travels? Okay, but He will probably primarily help with hangovers after you drink strange liquors. The same spell, cast with the assistance of Heimdall, on the other hand, will be more likely to help you stay alert to potential threats.

Each deity is a side of an infinitely large and infinitely faceted diamond. Our relationship with a given name or aspect allows us to begin to understand a vast and complex power, the Divine. We recognize that working with a name or aspect limits the nature of the Divine, but we need such a starting point to encompass the vastness of the Divine.[26] In short, our cosmology is dual: both narrow and infinite, personal and general.

One last thing about the nature of deities: while we might label given deities as male or female, those are human limitations imposed

---

26 A deity is never bothered by our inability to perceive their wholeness.

on something infinite in scope and power. Deities come in every form and aspect. There are deities with no gender and those with more than one. Some deities have no sexual activity (such as Artemis), and others have partners of multiple genders (such as Hermes). There may be times when the specific gender matters; for example, you might use a traditionally male deity and a traditionally female deity if you're trying to fortify your attempts to conceive a child with your partner. In general, however, gender matters less than you might think, more often than you think. Don't get caught up in biology; look for the energy of a name that seems most appropriate for the magic you want to accomplish. If a specific name doesn't attract you, sticking with a general "Divine One" is always polite and, with your words to describe your needs, will attract that which needs to come and assist your working. In my tradition, we open many rituals by inviting the Mother and the Father to join us; later, we might invoke particular aspects and names relevant to the work. That said, we encourage female-presenting participants to take male-presenting or oriented roles during a ritual while male-presenting members take female-presenting or oriented roles. None of us have ever received an indication that any of the deities we worked with have a problem when we do this.

Despite having put down on paper my feelings on the nature of relationships with the gods, I still honestly believe there is a place in this world for the spiritualist, the energy worker, the ritualist...whatever you want to call them, who practices everything that I do but never puts a name to the energy that they work with. It's a perfectly valid framework. For the non-theistic Witch, moving energy, connecting with others, and performing magic and rituals sits comfortably with them.[27] It does not matter that they have never felt a personified mind behind any of these workings. If your connection is to the energy that binds people together, it's not for me or anyone else to tell you that this is a connection to a deity. The connection is yours and yours alone; just like any significant relationship, you want to treat it respectfully. Granted, if you have no notion of personifying this existence, then the advice I offered about modeling your relationship isn't worth much.

27 A phrase I first saw used by John Halsted in his book, *Godless Paganism: Voices of Non-Theistic Pagans* (Lulu, 2016).

However, going about your business respectfully is still valuable, if only to maintain your mental health. There's nothing lost and plenty to be gained by infusing a part of your life with a positive outlook and an ongoing sense of getting along.

A Word About Cultural Appropriation

Cultural appropriation is a genuine and significant problem that may feel new to many of us but isn't. As with many societal issues, it's simply that a more significant percentage of the world is now aware of its existence. As such, I encourage you to read these descriptions, and if one of them sparks a response within you, don't take it as a signal to work with them immediately. Instead, begin learning more about them. For example, if you are intrigued by my description of Chalchihuitlicue, that's your cue to start answering questions like "why exactly was she the goddess of salt water? When would her worshippers pray to her? Were they asking for help or simply begging to be left alone as they traveled?" These things and more are what you'd want to know before involving her in your work. For example, Poseidon was said to be easily offended if ignored. If the Greek pantheon is something you work with, you would want to be aware of that, even if Poseidon is not a personal patron of yours. You're setting yourself up for trouble if you don't acknowledge him at the beginning of a cruise. This is an example of why learning everything you can is critical. If you're working with Hera, you're also working with Hera's family and friends, whether you plan to or not. "Better safe than sorry" has never been more appropriate.

All this being said, cultural appropriation can be a thorny subject. Some argue there is no place for taking on the practices of another culture, respectfully or otherwise. Others will say that doing so while showing due reverence is only bringing more people into the fold. You'll want to answer these questions satisfactorily; don't just brush them off.

I recommend giving more weight to answers from the community in question. I recently had to wrestle with the idea of learning about chakras being a form of appropriation. Investigating the issue, I found that practically all Hindus are happy for the information to spread; they are only displeased with the "dorm room poster" style of dissemination. Ultimately, we learned about chakras and their origins (almost guaranteed not to be what you've been taught) and then began energy work that created our own maps. When the culture of origin says they want us to work with their system (respectfully), we're on firmer ground. But it's an area to revisit regularly as you move deeper into your spiritual practice and further away from your comfort zone.

Travel Deities

Herewith is a list of twenty-three deities travelers have called upon over the centuries. These entries are necessarily brief, and I encourage you to delve into the rich mythologies of these deities for yourself.

- **Apollo (Greek):** God of archery, healing, light, medicine, and music. Usually depicted as a handsome young man with long hair, often holding a wreath and branch of laurel, kithara, or bow and quiver of arrows. His animals are the raven and the swan, and his plants are the laurel, larkspur, and cypress. Born on the seventh day of the seventh month, seven is his sacred number. As *Apollo Delphi,* he was petitioned for wisdom about where to create a new colony, making him a kind of patron to refugees and travelers heading for parts unknown. An incense offering to Apollo might consist of citron and frankincense.
- **Artemis (Greek):** Goddess of the hunt, forests, hills, and the Moon. Her symbols are bears, lions, bulls, sphinxes, bees, winged women, and the cypress tree. Most images of her depict a young woman dressed in a short hunting dress with boots, a quiver of arrows, and a bow. However, her statue at Ephesus (one of the Seven Wonders of the Ancient World) shows her with a flower wreath, zodiac necklace, lunar hairpiece, and a chest covered with breast-like lumps. An incense offering to Artemis might consist of cypress oil and myrrh.

- **Chalchihuitlicue (Aztec):** Goddess of salt water. She was usually depicted in a jade necklace, turquoise earrings, a crown of iridescent blue feathers with large tassels on either side of her face, and a skirt trimmed with lilies. She may have been honored at Teotihuacan in the cave under the Pyramid of the Sun, where a statue of her was found. After Christianization, she became Dona Maria Matlacoya, invoked in prayers for rain. An incense offering to Chalchihuitlicue might include jasmine, lavender, and lemon peel.
- **Chimata-no-kami (Japan/Shinto):** The "road-folk spirits" or "goddesses of innumerable roads," Chimata-no-kami are two guardians combined into one: *Yachimata-hime* and her consort, *Yachiamata-hiko.* They are usually depicted as two figures with arms around one another and holding hands. Travelers would petition their protection against ghosts, haunted buildings, demons, and other such specters. An incense offering to the Chimata-no-kami might consist of agarwood.
- **Diana (Roman):** Goddess of animals, chastity, fertility, hunting, the Moon, slaves, and woodlands. She is usually depicted as a young woman in a short hunting dress with boots, a quiver, and a bow. She is often accompanied by her sacred companions, a dog or stag; oak trees are especially sacred. During her festival on August 13 (some say 15), Roman women journeyed by torchlight to offer thanks for her help and to implore her continuing aid. Later, worship moved to Aventine Hill, where women flocked for ritual hair washing and invocations for safe childbirth. As *Diana Trivia,* she is the Goddess of three-way crossroads, protecting streets, roads, and avenues, particularly "Y" junctions. An incense offering to Diana might include jasmine, lemon, and myrrh.
- **Dōsojin (Japan/Shinto):** These "tutelary of roads" were found at village borders and intersections. Usually depicted as simple roundish stones, they sometimes look like young children or carved male or female genitals. Believed to guard against evil spirits and pestilence, their festival is held at the village border or a large road intersection on January 14. There, branches of

bamboo and green cedar are used to construct a large pillar or circular mass that is burned with various decorations and implements, including pine gate decorations and the papers used in New Year calligraphy contests. Eating rice cakes and confections roasted over the bonfire is believed to prevent sickness during the year and improve one's calligraphy and academic abilities. An incense offering to the Dōsojin might consist of agarwood.

- **Ekchuah/Ek Ahua (Mayan):** God of travelers. He is usually depicted as a dark-skinned man with a large lower lip, carrying a bag and spear. Travelers would stack three stones atop one another and offer incense at night to ensure a safe journey home. Cacao (cocoa) is sacred to him, and he was honored during Muwan, an annual festival held in April. An incense offering to Ekchuah might include mint and cacao.
- **Enodia (Greek):** Goddess of cemeteries, cities, ghosts, and roads. She was included in the local pantheon of goddesses alongside Hestia, Demeter, Aphrodite, Athena, and Themis. She sometimes shared sanctuaries with Zeus and is often conflated with Hecate. Her name (Goddess of the paths) suggests that she watched over entrances and stood on the main road into a city, keeping an eye on those who entered and on the road in front of private homes, protecting the inhabitants that dwelled within. Her image has been found on coins where she is seen as a young woman, riding a horse, carrying torches, with a dog at her side. An incense offering to Enodia might consist of oregano, thyme, and marjoram.
- **Ganesha (Hindu):** The remover of obstacles, elephant-headed and multiple-armed, with his trunk in a bowl of sweet delicacies, he is honored before all other deities in ceremonies and rituals. Ganesha is the patron of arts and sciences, intellect, and wisdom. His preferred offerings are sweets, seeds, and the color red. His primary festivals are the fourth day of the waxing moon in August/September and the fourth day of the waxing moon in January/February. An incense offering to Ganesh might include rose, rosemary, and lavender (alternatively, use dhoop, the traditional Hindu incense).

- **Gná (Norse):** Goddess of messages and swift travel. Frigg's personal messenger, she rides the horse Hófvarpnir (hoof-thrower), who can travel over both sea and sky. Depicted as a young woman with blonde hair and blue eyes, Gná was one of the Asynjur and wielded a spear. An incense offering to Gná might consist of sage and ginger.
- **Hecate (Greek):** Goddess of crossroads, entrances, ghosts, magic, and necromancy. Daughter of Titans, Hesiod wrote of how she assisted Demeter's search for Persephone by guiding her through the night while carrying torches. She kept two women transformed into animals: a black she-dog and a polecat. Usually depicted in typical women's garb, carrying two torches, she was sometimes dressed similarly to Artemis, in a knee-length maiden's skirt and hunting boots. As the daughter of the Titans, Hecate had power from the time before Zeus ruled and retained her dominion over the Earth, heavens, and sea. She walks the roads when the moon is dark, and her statues were found at the entrance to homes and wherever two roads cross. At the end of each month, dishes of food were put out at the crossroads to be consumed by those in need. Public sacrifices, usually at her festivals on August 13 and November 30, offered the goddess honey, black female lambs, dogs, and sometimes enslaved people. Her images were placed at the gates of cities and, eventually, domestic doorways. The Greeks planted poles crowned with masks of each of her three heads facing different directions at three-way crossroads. The Romans later called her *Hecate Trivia* after this three-way oversight. An incense offering to Hecate might include sandalwood, cypress, and mint.
- **Hermes (Greek):** God of astronomy, boundaries, commerce, diplomacy, herds, hospitality, language, music, roads, sports, thievery, travelers, and writing. He acted as Zeus' herald and messenger while enjoying the rare ability to enter and depart the Underworld at will. He is usually portrayed as a handsome, athletic young man, although older images show an older bearded man. He has a wide-brimmed hat, winged boots, and twin serpent-topped staff. His animals are the ram, hare, and hawk; his

plants are the strawberry and crocus. His sacred places are the herma, a stone road marker that doubled as a small wayside shrine. An incense offering to Hermes might consist of lavender, gum mastic, and saffron.

- **Iris (Greek):** Goddess of the rainbow and the messenger of the gods. Born of the sea and sky, she has no distinctive mythology. In myth, she appears only as an errand-running messenger and is usually described as a virgin goddess. Her name contains a double meaning, connected with the Greek word *iris,* "the rainbow," and *eiris,* "messenger." She is shown as a beautiful young woman with golden wings, a herald's rod (*kerykeion*), and sometimes a water-pitcher (*oinochoe*) in her hand, often standing beside Zeus or Hera, sometimes serving nectar from her jug. Homer, in *The Illiad,* describes her as assisting Achilles by calling the winds. Delians offered her cakes made of wheat and honey and dried figs. An incense offering to Iris might consist of lemon grass and ylang-ylang.
- **Janus (Roman):** God of gates, doors, doorways, beginnings, and endings. Depicted with two faces looking outward, the *ianua* (double-doored entrance), covered passages (*iani*), and the most important gates of a city are sacred to him. He presides over time itself and symbolizes change and transitions. His rituals took place at the beginning of every year and every month. As well, any rite or religious act required the invocation of Janus first, with a corresponding invocation to Vesta at the end. He prefers the morning. An incense offering to Janus might include mugwort, sandalwood, and orange peel.
- **Jizo Bosatsu (Japan/Buddhist):** This Bodhisattva vowed to protect women, children, and travelers. Depicted with a shaved head and a staff, his statues are common in cemeteries, often given a red cap or bib as a decoration. An incense offering to Jizo Bosatsu might consist of sandalwood, agarwood, and pine.
- **Khonsu (Egypt):** The god of travelers, he was depicted as a young man who traveled across the night sky, crowned by a rearing cobra and moon disk. The baboon and falcon are sacred to him. Sometimes referred to as the Pathfinder and the Defender, he

watched over travelers at night. An incense offering to Khonsu might include rose, mint, and ginger.

- **Mercury (Roman):** God of commerce, messages, and trade. Based on the Greek Hermes, he is similarly shown with winged sandals, a hat, and a staff. His holy day is May 15, and the cockerel, ram, and tortoise are sacred to him. An incense offering to Mercury might consist of mace, marjoram, and mint.
- **Neptune (Roman):** God of fresh water, often conflated with Poseidon and the sea. Usually depicted as a tall, white-bearded figure carrying a trident, he often has fish and horses with him. His festival was held on June 23 and celebrated water catchments and drainage. His animal is the dolphin, and his symbol is the trident. An incense offering to Neptune might consist of willow, orange, and ylang-ylang.
- **Njord (Norse):** God of fishing, sailing, wind, and the land along the seashore, often described as passive and effeminate in nature, there are no specific descriptions of how he looks. An incense offering to Njord might include anise, myrrh, and meadowsweet.
- **Poseidon (Greek):** God of the sea, earthquakes, floods, drought, and horses, his most common depiction is as a well-muscled mature man with a beard holding a trident (a three-pronged fisherman's spear). His animals are the bull, dolphin, and horse, but all sea creatures are in his domain. His plants are pine trees and wild celery. An incense offering to Poseidon might consist of pine, orange, and sandalwood.
- **Pushan (Hindu):** God of journeys, marriages, meetings, roads, and the Sun, he is symbolized by the Sun, his golden axe, his awl, and a chariot driven by goats. An incense offering to Pushan might consist of frankincense, desert sage, juniper, and cloves.
- **Terminus (Roman):** God of boundaries, his name is the Latin for boundary marker placed during a special ceremony that, if removed or damaged, would result in the culprit being slain. His festival (Terminalia) was held on February 23, when neighbors would decorate their boundary markers, leaving offerings of

honeycombs and wine for safety and protection in the coming year. An incense offering to Terminus might consist of honey, pine, star anise, and sage.

- **St. Christopher (Catholic):** Patron saint of travelers, especially for those undertaking journeys of longer distance and time, he is usually depicted as a strong older man carrying a (Christ) child. His feast day is July 25. Pilgrims on the Way of St. James to Santiago de Compostela in Northern Spain have traditionally carried scallop shells as a symbol of the saint and a reminder of God's protection. An incense offering to St. Christopher might include frankincense, myrrh, and copal or benzoin resin.

Finding a Deity for Your Journey

Even if you have a specific deity you work with, you may wish to also work with another during a particular journey. Here are two ways to reach out.

Altar Gathering

Create a generic altar or set aside space within your usual altar area at least a month before you leave, ideally at the new moon. Don't start with specific symbols, just a petition for guidance, using your own words. Over the next few weeks, spend time there daily contemplating whom you might feel drawn to or most appropriate. As you go through your ordinary life, look for signs and items that "speak" to you and your upcoming travels. At the full moon, look at what has accumulated: is there a pattern or connection?

Guided Meditation

Another way to connect with a deity as part of your upcoming journey is to do a specific meditation, usually called guided meditation, because the focus is not on clearing the mind but focusing with specific intent.

Begin by closing your eyes and spending a few minutes breathing (you may wish to follow the breathwork exercise in Chapter One). Relax your body as you breathe and allow yourself to enter a neutral state.

Imagine walking a path and coming upon a gate. Look at the gate for a moment, then open it, walk through, and close it behind you.

You stand at the edge of a beautiful meadow. Before you, scattered like gems, bloom wildflowers in all their glory. You see bluebells and buttercups, bee balm, and Queen Anne Lace. Coneflowers and Cornflowers. Bright poppies and daisies. Like a velvety blanket of color, the blooms raise their faces to the blue sky above. A gentle breeze caresses your hair and you smell the flowers. As you cross the meadow, the sun is warm on your face, following a faint trail. Enjoy this place as long as you wish.

Eventually, the path enters a wooded area. Tall trees tower above you here, leafy crowns offering shade and rustling in the breeze. Bird song is all around you, full of joy. You come to a small glade with a thick grass carpet, like velvet. Sit comfortably and ask, using your own words, for the guidance you desire.

After a bit, you are joined. Stand up and respectfully introduce yourself, politely awaiting a response (at this point, follow your intuition if possible and let events flow).

When you feel ready, offer your thanks and part. Return through the forest, through the verdant meadow, and the gate. There is no hurry; enjoy this place and the guidance you received. When you return, open your eyes, and feel your connection to the ground beneath you.

In my meditation, I envisioned myself in a peaceful meadow, connecting with the grounding energy of the earth. However, you can adapt this visualization to reflect your own personal journey. For instance, you may choose to wander along the shore of a vast sea, delving into its mysterious depths, or climb a mountain path and soar atop the back of a magnificent bird, exploring ethereal castles among the clouds. The beauty of this practice lies in its ability to be tailored to your unique experiences and desires.

Chapter Six

Magic by Location

When I first decided this would be a chapter in the book, its working title was "Cleaning out my Tome of Shadows." So much of this information began as lore that I either had gone looking for, intending to use it myself, or collected as it passed before my eyes, because it felt like something that I'd want someday. Maybe some tiny part of me in the back of my mind knew this book was coming; more likely, the fact that I'm the kind of person who likes to know these things helped to prompt my writing about it.[28]

Magic will work anywhere if our will and focus are strong enough. However, the power of places is often aligned with an element, allowing us to consider what kind of magic works best in specific areas. When we align ourselves with the natural energy of a place, working magic becomes more accessible and requires less effort.

- The *desert* is sacred to Fire and Air, an ideal location for clearing one's head, working on mediation, and contemplating the liminality of shifting sands.
- *Seashores* are sacred to Earth and Water, holding the ever-shifting and reforming edge within itself. This is an ideal place for magic involving emotions, divination, healing, and liminality.
- High in the *mountains* is sacred to Fire and Earth, a perfect choice for magic involving lifting oneself, seeking truth, and opening to abundance.
- *Caves* represent the fertile womb, sacred to Earth (or Water if a sea cave), and offer a place for dedicating an artistic project, becoming a new person, or starting over.

28 That said, some things I once took for granted are no longer a good idea, like collecting seashells to take home.

Some natural features are contained within these potent environments, allowing for powerful synergies to align.

- A *lightning-struck tree* holds the power of Fire within itself, offering a place for banishing work or rituals for survival. Such a tree in the mountains can redouble the Fire energy in that location, while the same tree in an open field allows easier access to Air.
- *Standing stones, menhirs, circles, alignments, dolmens, earthworks, and ruins* are all sacred to Earth. These sites have been found in numerous environments; they are often thought of in popular culture as standing alone in Northern Europe's cold, windswept hills. However, more and more archaeological work is being done yielding fantastic stone formations in the desert, and there is a site in Spain that is almost always submerged; recent droughts brought on by global climate change have had the (to be fair, mild) silver lining of revealing this fascinating location. Imagine what sort of innovative magic you might work on if you found yourself in a stone circle that spends almost all its time underwater.

Ancient sites must be greeted and honored before working within their surroundings. Consider: would you show up and hold a party at a neighbor's house uninvited? It's important to remember that many of these sites were employed for the same purpose you want to put them long before you ever came along, and effects can linger. Some places have nasty histories and are unsuitable for positive energy workings, so research before choosing a site. For example, Culloden, the battle site that meant the end of the Jacobite Rising in 1745, is evocative and eerie, as it is out on the Drummossie Moor in the Scottish Highlands. Despite its powerful imagery, the violent events and long-lasting fallout (regardless of your political sympathies) means I wouldn't recommend working magic under typical circumstances.

Some weather aligns with multiple elements, such as a rainstorm which is equally Air and Water. A gentle rain might still have a little Air to it, but I see it as primarily Water. A sunny day at the beach might bring you Fire and Water, while that same day in a cornfield can bring you Fire and Earth. Don't forget that you don't have to use all available elements, although the strong presence of one can make it harder to tune it out. That sunny day at the beach could still be helpful to you in a spell that wants Fire but no Water at all; the ocean would be incidental in that case. Of course, that same spell done while standing up to your chest in the water is likely harder to keep separate. There are also your associations and connections to consider: if you do not enjoy the seashore, for example, trying to do magic there will work against itself. Whatever you read in a book, mine or any other, will never outdo the strong associations you've already formed.

Sometimes you don't have a choice about the location; that's true more often than it isn't for many of us. Consider how you can boost the spell to overcome that negative input.[29]

Inviting the Powers

This is a general outline, easily modified to suit your surroundings, and can be done whether you have a formal altar, a traveling version, or just items you find out of need (the below presumes you have a feather, a lit candle, a water container, and a rock. Substitute other items or use your imagination to create the best representations possible).

Take three breaths and calm yourself. Consider your intent clearly and think it through as thoroughly as possible. Face East and hold the feather in your non-dominant hand. Say (either aloud or clearly in your mind):

"I invite the powers of Air to join me in this rite/spell
Bringing their inspiration, freshness, and clarity
Together we shall co-create this working
By our will, so mote it be!"

Feel the arrival of Air, the freshening breeze, a wind sweeping through you, a dazzling sky, no matter that it is entirely within your head.

29 This can be as easy as a reframing. If your ferry service is on strike, then using your reluctance to be seaside can power the spell to get home.

When Air is present, return the feather to your altar and turn to the South. Hold your receptive hand over the candle flame, close enough to feel the warmth but not to harm you. Say (either aloud or clearly in your mind):

"I invite the powers of Fire to join me in this rite/spell
Bringing their transformation, passion, and singularity
Together we shall co-create this working
By our will, so mote it be!"

Feel the arrival of Fire, a roaring bonfire, a crackling campfire, the comfort of the kitchen oven, love of family, friends, or your partner.

When Fire is present, turn to the West and pick up the water container. Say (either aloud or clearly in your mind):

"I invite the powers of Water to join me in this rite/spell
Bringing their healing, purification, and guarantee
Together we shall co-create this working
By our will, so mote it be!"

Feel the arrival of Water, the sound of rainfall, the ocean waves, the taste of clear water in your mouth, of swimming.

When Water is present, return the container to your altar and turn North. Hold the rock in your receptive hand. Say (either aloud or clearly in your mind):

"I invite the powers of Earth to join me in this rite/spell
Bringing their strength, firm footing, and prosperity
Together we shall co-create this working
By our will, so mote it be!"

Feel the arrival of Earth, the land's fertility, the rock's strength, and its millennia-long endurance.

When Earth is present, return the rock to your altar. Hold your hands above the items, feeling the pulse of their power and willingness to work with you. Move your hands in a clockwise motion over the items, saying:

"Hail and welcome Elemental Beings!
Fill me with your magic power
Enfold me in your arcane might
Together we manifest in this hour!"

You are ready to proceed with your ritual or spell.

Earth Power

The earth is the foundation upon which we stand. For many, it is the Mother from which we all come. Hidden by weather in winter, eagerly nourishing seeds in spring, bountifully producing life-giving sustenance before shedding the glorious foliage in autumn, earth's seasonal cycle offers many lessons for us. This is the energy of stability, reliability, durability, and abundance. Almost any travel situation can utilize the power of Earth; think of it like a constantly available battery for you to tap into.

Safe Return Binding Spell

Based on a book-binding ritual by Scott Cunningham, this spell is excellent for when you or a loved one is on a long journey. Bindings and knots are physical representations of intangible goals powered by personal energy.

You will need:

- A length of cord about 12" in length
- The person traveling or the luggage going on the journey

Take three breaths and calm yourself. Consider your intent clearly and think it through as thoroughly as possible. Hold the hand of the person or the luggage between your palms, saying:

"By hill and wind, flame and brook
Under shining Moon and upon the sea,

I place a bind upon [name] (alt: this suitcase)
That it will absolutely return to me."

Wrap the cord around their hand (or the handle), securing it with a knot so you can slip it off without untying it. As you tie the knot, visualize the person or suitcase returning to you, and repeat:

"By hill and wind, flame and brook
Under shining Moon and upon the sea,
I place a bind upon [name] (alt: this suitcase)
That it will absolutely return to me."

Slip off the knotted cord and put it in a secret place. When they leave for travel, or you say goodbye, wish them well, and repeat the words of the chant (even if it's under your breath). Once they return, untie or cut the cord.

Stone Divination

Find three stones, one dark, one light, and one of a unique color different from the other two. Choose which stone will represent the answers yes and no; the uniquely colored stone will be the significator. Hold the three stones in your hand while you take three deep breaths and contemplate your intent. Ask a simple yes/no question. Shake the stones in your hands and throw them onto the ground or a table in the center of the area. This stone which is closest to the significator answers the question.

If one of the stones falls off a raised area, there is no answer to be had. Similarly, no answer is forthcoming if the yes and no stones are the same distance from the significator stone. In either case, try again later.

When not using them, keep the stones in a pouch out of sight and let no one else touch them.

Flower Divination

Choose a flower at random, but do not pick it. Take three deep breaths and contemplate your intent. Ask a simple yes/no question, then count the petals, saying yes or no until you reach the last petal, which is your answer. Do not pluck the petals; there is no need to destroy the flower to get the answer.

Air Power

Air energy is light and can feel like any temperature when you work with it. It is most potent during storms, with the wind blowing strongly, and the energy is even more intense if there is lightning. Air energy tends to be most beneficial for divination to clarify a situation or for inspiration in problem-solving.

On the day your journey begins, check the wind. If it comes from the east, that is a good sign; if from the north, be cautious during your travels for unexpected issues to arise. (If from the south or west, the omens are generally favorable). When you return home, the winds are most favorable from the west and neutral from the east or south.

Aid in Decision-Making

Use the energy of the east wind to help if you feel overwhelmed with too many choices.

You will need:

- A slip of paper for each option
- Table or another flat surface
- Access to the outdoors where a gentle wind is blowing

Ideally, the wind is coming from the east. Write each option on a slip of paper and fold twice. When finished, gather all the pieces of paper in your two hands and go outside to your table. Take three deep breaths and say aloud:

"Wind of East, hear my call
Which choice is best, of them all?"

The wind will (or should) make the papers move around and eventually fall to the ground. Remember your request for assistance while the pieces are being sifted through. The choice is the last paper left (or to fall to the ground if you don't catch it in time).

Rain's End Charm

An old charm for checking if the rain has stopped falling looks to the local birds. If they fly around, not just perch on branches, or make short hops, it's a good sign the rain has stopped.

Watching them, say aloud:

"Swift-winged flyers in the air
Flit about without a care.
I ask of you:
Will it rain here or there?"

If they fly away, track the direction.

- **East:** it will remain clear.
- **South and West:** there is more rain coming.
- **North:** it will remain clear, but until sunset.

Generating a Journey Spell

Paper airplanes are fantastic for manifesting travel. While I use an airplane as an example, you can use any shape, such as a train or boat.

You will need:

- A sheet of paper
- A pencil or other writing instrument
- A needle
- Thread

Take three breaths and calm yourself. Consider your intent clearly and think it through as thoroughly as possible. When you feel ready, write on the paper exactly where you want to go, visualizing it as clearly as possible. Say "Barcelona" rather than "Spain," or "Riviera Maya" instead of "Mexico." Add images supporting your destination (an outline of La Sagrada Familia or a bougainvillea flower, for example). Fill in the paper (write very large to fill the space). When you are finished, hold the paper in your projective hand and visualize yourself there.

Fold the paper into an airplane shape using the technique I show below or your preferred design. The only important rule is that the plane must be able to fly. You want it to go several feet, at least, before coming to rest. (If you aim upward rather than down or horizontally, it goes further).

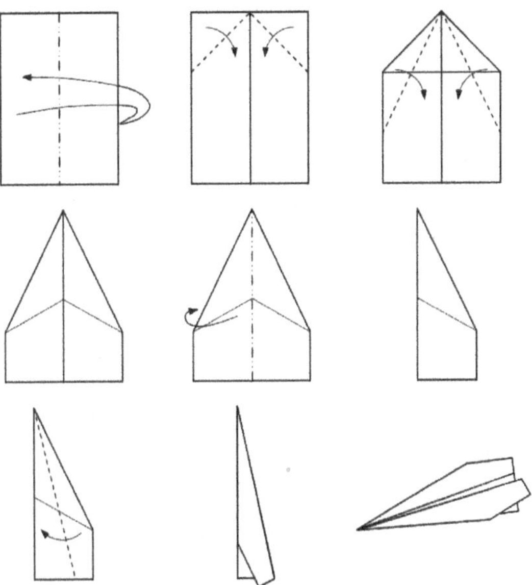

Paper Airplane Instructions

While folding the paper airplane, visualize your journey. Feel yourself at your destination and consider what you'll do while there.

Don't think about any problems or obstacles to your ability to go on the journey, just the successful enjoyment.

With the completed airplane in hand, go outside. Take three breaths and calm yourself, then launch the plane into the air (this is super fun from a high window).

Retrieve the plane from where it lands. Thread the needle, then pierce the nose and tail to hang it from the ceiling. Leave it suspended until it's time to leave on your journey, then take the plane with you. When you return from your trip, tear the paper into small pieces and recycle it.

AIR SPELL

A lovely spell for when the leaves have just started to fall in the autumn.

You will need:

- A fallen leaf that is still pliable (they crumble too easily when dried)
- A pen

On a day when the wind is blowing strongly, go to the highest place outside that you can manage. On the leaf, draw a symbol of what you want to manifest.

Holding the leaf in your hands, close your eyes and merge with the power of Air, feeling the wind as if you are the same. Visualize your desire clearly and in as much detail as possible. When it feels right, toss the leaf high into the air. The spell is complete if the wind catches it and blows it away from you. If it does, try the spell again, at most three times. If it continually fails, take it as a sign that you are asking for too much, for something too complicated, or that your desire will not be granted.

FIRE POWER

Fire energy is devouring and, therefore, challenging to work with under normal circumstances. This is the energy of sexuality, desire, will, energy, and destruction. When traveling, Fire energy is found in all engines and during the part of the day when the Sun is at its height.

ENERGY BOOST SPELL

Some days we all need more energy than we usually have available.

You will need:

- A piece of paper
- A pen, ideally with red ink

On a sunny day, draw an image of a many-rayed sun on the paper. Place the image in full sunlight (weigh it down with small stones on the corners to keep it from blowing away) for at least an hour. Once the paper has been charged and packed with the sun's energy, pick it up with your receptive (non-dominant) hand. All that energy is now within you.

One of the most enduring temples within the Roman Forum is the Temple of Vesta, where a colonnade of statues, each different, leads to the house they shared as part of their duties. Walking the sacred precincts, I felt a strong connection to those long-ago priestesses, leading me to wonder whether a past-life connection existed.

Star Magic

The delight of a night sky, unpolluted by light, is one every person should see at least once. One of my college science courses was astronomy, which included a lab. So up we went to the top of the engineering building, two nights a week, to look through telescopes and peer at assignments with flashlights taped over with red cellophane. I learned how to estimate the time, read a star chart, and do other general tasks.

It was also when I began to work with the power of starlight. These tiny suns are vast containers of fire energy, available anytime there is a clear sky.

Star Bath

Best done when it's warm; you do not need to be naked to enjoy it. Sit or lie beneath a clear night sky and lower any habitual shields you wear. Bathe in the brilliant white-tinged-with-blue light pouring down upon you. Feel its warmth; let it relax your muscles, relaxing you, infusing you with energy. Contemplate the truth that stars are far away suns that affect us and our world, just as the planets do.

Power of the Stars Spell

This is not a spell for a specific outcome but a way to power a spell you create. Before you begin, contemplate how star energy is the best to power your spell and how it aligns with your intent. You may wish to write your intent on a piece of paper to be burned later.

Cast your circle and invite the Beings and Powers. Visualize a vast field of stars glowing all around you, bright against the deep darkness of the void. You are surrounded by infinity. When you feel ready, pick a star, and move towards it. As you approach, stretch forth your hands and take in the star's energy as much as you can comfortably hold. You do not need to get too close or continue past the point of pain from the energy you absorb. You're not impressing anyone. Hold the power gathered, a warm bundle of star energy, within your hands as you return to your physical self. Pour it onto the paper (if using) or fling it up and out as you concentrate on your intent.

Candle Magic

Candle magic is an excellent way to work with Fire and is one of the most customizable and accessible ways to work magic. While it might be a little more complicated when traveling, you can often find candles in local stores. Look for small stores in neighborhoods called *bodegas* in San Francisco's Mission District and *mercearia* here in Portugal. Décor and "dollar" stores can provide colored candles, usually in handy glass dishes. It may be a little bit of an adventure, but if a candle spell is what you want to do, the supplies are available.

Colored candles add energy and focus to your spell, but basic white will always be appropriate. If using color, use the one that means the most to you rather than relying on the correspondences others have created. To give you an idea of what I mean, pink is the color of choice for love spells, according to almost every list I have come across, but I do not like pink. Really, honestly, *do not like it.* Using that color would almost certainly work entirely against the spell's energy.

If I have time and a bit of oil, I prefer to dress (or anoint) my candles before using them for magic. Many places I've stayed in that have a kitchen also have cooking basics, like salt, pepper, and oil. Your oil doesn't need to be fancy; plain vegetable oil works great.

To anoint a taper candle to bring something *in* to your life, dip the fingers of your dominant hand in the oil and stroke them from the top of the candle to the middle, working all around.[30] Turn the candle upside-down and repeat from the bottom to the middle. To use the candle to keep something out, or *let go* of something from your life, rub the oil from the middle to the top and bottom. If you have small round candles (like tealights), rub the oil in a clockwise direction to bring energy in and counterclockwise to push or release

30 Yes, you can make a circle of your first finger and thumb and pull the candle through, but your mind might go to sexual imagery, or you'll have a fit of giggles, and that may not be the purpose of your spell. If it is, do that instead of the method I describe.

it away. No matter what shape the candles are, while drawing your fingers over the candle, tell it your magical intention. You are making an ally of the candle, so do your best to feel the energetic connection.

My travel altar kit contains a tapestry needle so I can carve appropriate symbols into the candle, which adds to the spell's power. While not strictly necessary, these symbols are another personal connection, and they can be created from words, images, runes, or whatever you desire.

Ensure your candle can burn safely on a flat surface and will not be unattended. Many hotels do not allow anything to be burned, like candles or incense, because of fire hazards. Don't violate their rules; it's rude, and frankly, working energy illicitly is getting things off on the wrong foot. Think of our work on correspondences earlier; you are adding "I shouldn't be doing this" and "I am being a bad guest" to whatever other sentiments you are working with, which is a recipe for failure. You will leave the candle to burn out if possible or pinch it out after an appropriate period. Relight it and let it burn at least three nights in a row if you can't let it burn out. Some people feel very strongly about never blowing out their candle; they believe it "blows away" the energy. This has not been the case for me, but it is something you may wish to discover for yourself.

Safety note: be careful of how hot your candleholder gets; it may damage the surface it sits on. When in another's home, I try to place the candle on a stone surface or in a dish of sand or dirt. Also, some holders are wobbly, so make sure the candle won't fall over. Fire is always dangerous, but preparation and careful consideration will ameliorate the potential issues.

While candle magic is best done at night (as is true for most spellwork), it still works during the day. To light the candle, strike your match and lower it slowly, with intent, to the wick, all the while understanding that the match is the spark of Fire that you bring to set your spell (the candle) into motion. Ideally, you can drop the match into a flame-proof container to let it go out on its own, but that's not possible, blow it out with thanks for its contribution to your magic. Spend time visualizing your spell's successful outcome as you watch the candle flame.

SIMPLEST CANDLE SPELL

Start with your intention: what do you want to bring about? Set up your work area, ensuring it is safe and the candle can burn undisturbed until it burns out. Choose your candle. State your intention and light the candle. Allow it to burn out.

Everything else you might do—herbs, stones, anointing, etc.—is an additional energetic booster.

MIRROR MAGIC

Mirrors are old magic based on the reflective surfaces found in the still waters of nature with the additional power from the fire of the furnace and an alignment with the Moon, which reflects the power of the Sun.

I've often carried a mirror for on-the-spot negativity reversals while traveling. Classically, a Witch's mirror is between thirteen and thirty inches in diameter and encased in a round frame, painted black.[31] My mirror is square, about three inches on each side, and encased in a silver compact, like for makeup, and I keep it in a black cotton case when not used. It's easy to travel with and unobtrusive.

To prepare your mirror for magical use, wash its face carefully with a weak tea of an herb associated with psychic gifts. Mugwort is typical, but alternates include bay, jasmine, lemongrass, and vervain.[32] Wrap it in black cloth made of a natural material until the full moon. That night, uncover the face of the mirror to the Moon's light and place it on a flat surface. Doing this outdoors is best, but an open window or doorway will also work.

Hold your hands over the reflective face so that your dominant hand goes clockwise and your non-dominant hand goes counterclockwise.

---

31 Scott Cunningham, *Cunningham's Book of Shadows* (Llewellyn Publications, 2008) 167.

32 I use one tablespoon of herb steeped in three cups of hot water steeped for nine minutes then strained and cooled before using. I make a fresh batch for every working; it doesn't keep for more than a few days.

Hand Motions for Mirror Preparation

While doing these movements, chant:

"Power of the moon tonight
smiling down on me
I connect myself to infinity
Capturing the moon's power so bright.

The cycle of moonlight is caught within
I connect to the cycle of infinity
The moon's power caught in this silver disk
Moon smiling down on me
I stand in the moon's light tonight
It is shining down on me
I connect to the cycle of infinity
In the moonbeams so bright."

Draw circles with your hands at least three times but repeat more often if it feels correct. Wrap it until you wish to use it. Repeat this energetic charging three times a year, and do not use this mirror for mundane tasks.

Tiny mirrors, like those in some garments or jewelry, are fantastic for protection. Empowered to "bounce back" negativity, they are best cleansed (using the tea mentioned above) and recharged at the full moon after each wearing.

All mirrors in your home should be blocked so they cannot be used as a doorway into this world. This is done as efficiently as cleaning them monthly with a bit of vinegar (which is also an excellent cleaner). Any mirror in the house can be empowered as a protector. Cleanse and charge them, as above, and ask them to absorb negativity, guarding against evil in all forms.

I was hanging out in a café in Barcelona while my husband went on an errand. People-watching is great, but the vibe went wrong when I noticed a creepy guy a few tables away watching me. Nothing subtle about it. I deliberately made eye contact and then looked away dismissively; he only smiled slightly (more like a smirk) and kept watching me. "He's working a malefic on me," I thought, realizing that something I'd only read about until then was happening to me. I checked my shields, and sure enough, they were being eaten away by an outside force coming from his direction. I pulled my mirror out of my backpack and held it. I opened my connection to a deity and asked for protection, that the mirror reflect precisely what he was sending me. I then opened the mirror and placed it on the table, the reflective side toward him.

As I ordered another café, I reinforced my shields. Within minutes, he was blinking rapidly, shaking his head as if a fly was buzzing around him. Not long after that, he (at a quick glance) looked quite pale, and a waiter asked him if he was feeling well. While I didn't understand the entire exchange, I understood that a sudden headache had come over him, and no, he wasn't feeling well. He left, stumbling a bit, right after that. When I saw that, I took up my mirror and thanked the deity for its protection. That night I washed the mirror with a bit of salt mixed in water, dried it carefully, and put it away.

Burning Away Evil Spell

Mirrors, like the magnifying glasses we played with in childhood, are great for setting things on fire. This spell takes advantage of that in a satisfactory way, although it requires a sunny day.

You will need:

- A mirror
- A piece of paper or birch bark
- Writing instrument and ink
- Flameproof dish

Sit quietly and take three deep breaths. Contemplate your specific intent and then write it on the paper or bark before placing it in the dish.

Position the mirror to catch the sun's rays and reflect them onto the paper. It will take a bit, but once it catches fire, say:

"Energy of the sun, and in [deity]'s name![33]
Thy power is thwarted, up in flames!
No more will you bother me, or mine
Begone! You are banished, and I shine!"

Break A Mirror Spell

Broken mirrors are harbingers of bad luck (seven years is a common thought), but a deliberately broken mirror offers a powerful bit of magic.

You will need:

- A small mirror
- A large rock

33 [Deity] refers to the specific name, if you are using one. If you don't work with a specific deity, you can substitute a more neutral "in God's (or Goddess's) name," or even "in my name"!

Hold the mirror in your projective (dominant) hand and visualize your problem—the person, situation, obstacle, or habit—clearly and with detail. Place the mirror on a hard surface, ideally not in your house (be thoughtful about the placement, you'll want to gather up all the broken pieces and leave the place scrupulously clean when finished). Ensure your image is never reflected as you place the mirror on the ground. Carefully position the rock and let it drop onto the glass, shattering it and your problem (clean carefully and dispose of the pieces and rock in the garbage. This is best for the dump, not burial).

Water Power

Most people find Water energy the easiest to work with, whether from a faucet or a river. Its energies are that of emotions, psychic powers, and divination, and this is the element of absorption and movement.

Simple Water Divination

Hold a pebble in your projective hand and consider your yes/no question (keep it simple without parenthetical phrases). Drop the pebble into a pool of water and count the rings. An odd number of rings is yes; an even number means no (a glass of water will do, but it can be hard to count quickly enough, I find a shallow bowl works well).

Wishing Well Magic

I have no idea where I first learned this spell, but I suspect it came from a fairy tale. If you come upon a wishing well (or fountain or natural spring regularly cleaned), make a wish and toss a coin into it.

A specific version for money has you energizing the coin by chanting:

"Coin of metal, bright and shiny
Bring me lots of money!"

Then toss the coin into the well.

Working with Fog

Growing up in San Francisco, the fog was a powerful ally in my magic. I lived in the Mission District, an area surrounded by hills, and remembering how the fog would surge over the crest and down the slopes is a powerful touchstone for me. Fog blurs the physical world, making the astral plane easier to access.

If fog surrounds you while traveling, it might disrupt many plans. Instead of giving in to worry or anger, use its power. Step outside into the fog and open your arms in a welcoming gesture. Into the fog directly in front of you, project your desired outcome, and see it happening as vividly as you can manage. Step into that bit of fog when you have finished and feel its energy within yourself. Thank the fog for making your desire a reality while closing your arms.

Stormy Weather

Generally speaking, spells done during stormy weather will end up supercharged as the environment often becomes full of the power of Water, Air, and Fire. I like to access the energy of a storm to charge my travel talismans and charms, using what typically turns into an enforced "down day" for a positive magical purpose. The easiest way to do this is by placing them outside to absorb the energy. A few caveats: make sure they can get wet and won't draw lightning. Do what you need to keep them safe and intact during the charging process. My fabric bundle of stones and herbs might turn into a rotting mess if it gets wet, as an illustration. In this case, I would take the herbs out before putting the bundle outside. When it dried out, I'd add the herbs back, using the original chant.

It was my last summer before leaving home to go to college, and I was with family on the Jersey Shore. The storms there are incredible as they come across the ocean, lightning alternating between jagged forks touching the sea and sheeting across the sky. The air is charged with energy, an extraordinary force to tap into. I went outside the house and watched the storm approach from the safety of the area under the upper-floor deck, considering how I wanted to use this energy. Feeling my intention clarify, I stepped out into the rain and held my arms up to the sky, hands open and inviting:

"Storm-wrought power, I call to thee.
Grant my desire, I ask of thee.
My wish do grant, asked by three,
As I will so mote it be!"

I called loudly and strongly into the air, visualizing meeting other Witches when I left home. I wanted a teacher and others to explore Witchcraft and magic with. I wanted more than I could find on my own, and I wanted it so badly I could feel it like a pain within my body. The storm's energy picked up intensity as I chanted three times; when I dropped my arms to bow in thanks the final time, the rain abruptly stopped.

Within a few months of arriving at college, I found the group I worked with through most of my time there.

Sea Magic

The power of the ocean is entrancing and ancient. Many of our ancestors lived near the ocean, which provided them with a rich source of sustenance, trade with other cultures, and magic. In a pinch or as preparation for sea travel, a bowl of water with sea salt added can substitute for the actual ocean.

Tidal Energy

The tides are the breath of the ocean and, like the Moon, have three primary phases offering additional energy to our magic:

- **Incoming:** When the tide comes in, moving from low to high. This time is best for productive spells that draw in specific energy, such as fertility, healing, abundance, and protection.
- **High:** The tide's highest point in any given twelve-hour period. Suitable for any magical work, whether drawing in or pushing out. A genuinely auspicious point for magic is during the highest tide within a month.
- **Ebbing:** When the tide goes out, moving from high to low.

Low tide, the opposite of high tide, is best used for introspection rather than magic. There are two peaks and nadirs daily, so check the tides online through a site like Tideschart.[34]

Taking seashells home to remember our experience is tempting, but it's not a good idea. Leaving seashells where they are is one of the easiest ways to protect marine life and make a small contribution to saving our oceans. There is a wide variety of plants and animals that depend on empty shells for their survival. The most well-known example is the hermit crab, which uses spiral shells for their homes. As they grow, they must find a larger shell to move into, or they die from exposure or predation. But other creatures, like barnacles, limpets, and

34 "World Tide Times, Tide Tables, and Tide Charts." *Tidescharts,* 2025, www.tideschart.com/World-Tides.

chitons, make their homes on top of empty shells. Seagrasses, corals, and anemones anchor themselves to the ocean floor with shells; small fish use discarded shells for cover and shelter. Birds and some marine animals use shells as building material for their nests.

One person taking a shell doesn't negatively impact the environment. But anytime humans, in their huge numbers, engage in an activity, we affect our environment. Usually for the worse. Think of it like this: if every person who walks by your home took a handful of dirt, likely thinking to themselves, "what harm will one handful do?", what would that look like? In the beginning, it's no big deal. Eventually, however, you'll notice problems like your grass eroding or a giant hole forming.

Seashells found in stores are usually collected from live animals, and the practice is devastating to marine wildlife.[35] The shells are harvested with live occupants because they are pristine, and their color quickly fades when empty (just the thought creeps me out). I encourage you to take pictures instead of physical items.

If you want to use seashells for magic, tapping into their ancient legacy of power, you can return them before you leave the area. Alternatively, use them to create a circle in the sand to contain the energy you raise but don't take them with you. Long, spiral-shaped shells connect more easily to gods, while round ones link us to goddesses.

Use a piece of driftwood to create your sacred circle or draw symbols of your magical intent for the sea to absorb. Watch the ocean and meditate on your intent, visualizing your need. Consider which images and symbols best express your intent (anything is suitable, including writing out what you want in detail). As you watch the ocean, let the waves resonate within you and feel power begin to build. When you feel ready, draw your symbols above where the ocean is coming in and hold the energy. Just as a wave sweeps up to your symbols,

---

35 Marc Mancini, "Where Have All the Seashells Gone?" *Howstuffworks,* 16 Apr. 2024, science.howstuffworks.com/environmental/earth/oceanography/where-have-all-seashells-gone.htm; Tina Deines, "The Seashell Trade for Souvenirs is Killing Protected Marine Life," *National Geographic,* 16 Jul. 2018, www.nationalgeographic.com/animals/article/wildlife-watch-seashells-illegal-trade-handicrafts; Vincent Nijman, "Souvenirs, Shells, and the Illegal Wildlife Trade," *Journal of Ethnobiology,* vol. 39, no. 2, 4 May 2023, p. 282, www.researchgate.net/publication/3338265.

release the energy. Thank the powers and leave, knowing your desire will be fulfilled.

Holed stones were once seen as gifts of the sea and have many magical properties. However, like seashells, taking them is no longer one I can recommend. If you have one, you can string it on a cord and hang it in your home for protection and good luck.

Swimming in the ocean can cleanse you of negativity, much like when we ground excess energy into the earth.

Snow and Ice Magic

The first snowfall of the season is magical in many ways. The world grows quiet, almost as if holding its breath. Adults play like children, and children run wild with excitement. We all indulge a little if we can, brewing up pots of cocoa and making special treats to celebrate the season.

Growing up in San Francisco, we never saw snow beyond a light sprinkle that burned away with the sunrise, and there were only a few family vacations to places where real snow fell. It wasn't until I lived in New York City that snow became part of my winter life and I learned to work with it. It wasn't until I lived in the Pacific Northwest that I began to work with Ice as a separate energy from Snow.

Snow Figure Manifestation Spell

This spell requires several inches of relatively fresh snow.

Before going out, contemplate your intent and visualize it. When you feel your goal is fixed clearly in your mind, go outside and find a place where the snow is undisturbed and likely to remain that way. Draw a symbol of your desire into the snow with the index finger of your dominant hand (or a stick), visualizing your desired intent.

SNOW CHARM FOR PROTECTION

Snow can be dangerous in many ways; this charm helps the wearer keep safe. You can use any mixture of spices or substitute any dried herb that has protective qualities. Ideally, the cloth and thread will be red.

You will need:

- A pinch each of salt and three "warming" spices (such as turmeric, ginger, pepper, or nutmeg)
- A bowl
- Piece of cloth, cut in a circle about 4" in diameter
- Needle and thread

Sit quietly and take three deep breaths. Put the salt into the bowl, saying aloud: *"I charge you with stability!"*

Put the first of the spices into the bowl, saying aloud: *"I charge you with protection!"*

Put the second of the spices into the bowl, saying aloud: *"I charge you with protection!"*

Put the last of the spices into the bowl, saying aloud: "I charge you with protection!"

Mix the spices and salt with your fingers, visualizing the wearer enjoying themselves outside, walking safely, moving easily, and keeping perfectly warm in the snow. Transfer the mixture to the center of the cloth. Fold the cloth over the spice/salt mix, then fold again. Sew the edges so that the mixture can't fall out. Carry as needed and dispose of with spring's arrival.

Don't Panic! Coping with (Inevitable) Trouble

Sometimes you must travel in a hurry, without time to make a charm bag or work a formal spell. No worries, there are almost always items around you can use at the last minute.

- **Soap:** Those little bars in hotel rooms can be charged as an amulet to protect against negativity.
- **Mints:** Found in almost every shop and airport kiosk, mints are great to charge to create clearer communication or to sweeten an official's disposition toward you.
- **Matches:** While less common in the United States, many places in the European Union still allow smoking and offer matches to patrons. A book of matches offers a great charm to banish darkness (negativity) or bring illumination.
- **Napkins:** Paper napkins are perfect for writing out charms to smooth your journey (while poetry is fun, a heartfelt petition always offers energy to pour forth). Here's a super quick protection charm: Write your full name and birthdate on a paper napkin. Write the word "protect" on all four sides, surrounding your name and birthdate completely. Fold the napkin nine times and tuck it into a pocket until you arrive safely.
- **Snacks:** Snacks containing garlic and other herbs can be consumed (after charging and with intent) to bring you protection and their magical properties.
- **Salt:** Salt mixed with water is a fantastic cleansing and protection agent.

Fast Petition Charms

I first got the idea for petition charms from Cal Garrison, who wrote about using sticky notes wrapped in a thread for spellwork. Like the Fast Sigil Charm (above), using paper notes is a quick way to raise and focus power. This isn't a specific technique so much as a method, and I encourage you to change it up and do your own version.

You can use paper napkins, a page from your journal, notepaper, or whatever you can get your hands on. Depending on how much room you have, write out your petition, repeating the words at least three times (and up to nine). If you can make the words rhyme, great, but it's not required to make this spell successful.

Place the paper under a candle if you are at home, or it's easy to make happen. Burn the candle while concentrating on your petition. If a candle can't be managed, hold the paper in your dominant hand and push your energy into it.

Your petition paper can travel with you, or you can burn or destroy the petition paper as part of your spell. Hold the petition paper after the candle burns to keep the energy going. You can also add that petition paper to a new spell.

First Aid

Getting a premade first aid kit at a drugstore is often possible, but they are usually very large for those of us who travel a lot and want to stick with the smallest and lightest bags possible. Several years ago, I developed a first aid kit that fits in a prescription pill bottle. Supplemented by a few packets of herbs, most of my immediate emergency needs are quickly taken care of, at least long enough to get more substantial assistance.

Pocket First Aid Kit

Into a prescription pill bottle (cleaned, with the label removed), place the following:

- Antibiotic ointment (such as Neosporin)
- Band-Aids (3–4)
- Tweezers
- Safety pins (1–2)
- Toothache reliever (such as Orajel)
- Ibuprofen (6–8 pills)
- Diarrhea medication (such as Imodium, 3–4 pills)

Wrap the pills in a bit of parchment or waxed paper, clearly labeled, to keep them dry. Between trips, swap them out to make sure they don't expire.

The herbs I bring are folded in parchment or waxed paper, keeping them dry for several weeks. My usual herbal pharmacopeia comprises chamomile, lemon balm, peppermint, and vervain. Most people like lavender (which I loathe), but I will bring it for my husband. Chamomile, lavender, and peppermint are often easily found in the herbal tea blends of grocery stores. Check out your local and chain coffee shops if that comes up short (I've purchased tea without hot water on several occasions just to get the herbs).

General dosage: 1–2 tsp of blended herbs, depending on the cup size and how strong you like your tea. Steep for five to ten minutes and strain before drinking.

Uplift Herbal Tea

This blend does not wake you up so much as lift your spirit and assist in creating a state of mellow relaxation.

- One part each: chamomile, vervain, lavender, lemon balm
- Two parts peppermint

Relaxing Herbal Tea

Excellent at the end of the day to ease towards sleep.

- Two parts each: lemon balm, chamomile

If my throat feels tight or sore, I head to the local grocery and buy some common sage and rosemary. After steeping it in hot water for ten minutes, I'll gargle with it for a day.

PRACTICAL MAGIC: HELP WHILE TRAVELING

Traveling outside your home country always carries an element of risk, and sometimes you'll find yourself too far outside your comfort zone. Magic and alternative remedies only go so far; you must support your energetic work with practical, physical world action.

The U.S. State Department offers twenty-four-hour assistance seven days a week for United States citizens engaged in international travel. They can be reached through the nearest U.S. Consulate or Embassy on their website or via phone at the Washington D.C. office (888-407-4747 or 202-501-4444). Similar assistance exists for countries within the European Union.

The U.S. State Department also offers a free program, the Smart Traveler Enrollment Program (STEP), which provides travel and security updates to enrollees. If an extreme situation arises, such as a war, they will have the information to reach and guide you to safety.

The most common security issues for travelers are getting scammed, being robbed, and falling ill or suffering an accident. All these issues are horrible, but dealing with them in a foreign country where most of us have no support network makes it worse.

If something illegal happens to you, your priority is to get to safety. Any *thing* can be replaced, but you are unique and irreplaceable. Find a police station, hospital, medical center, or large hotel. If pertinent, get medical attention. Only then consider whether you will report it to the local police.

Making the issue public is cringe-worthy for some of us, almost as bad as the initial violation. However, in some countries failing to report a crime is, in and of itself, a crime. If your car is stolen and the thief uses it in a carjacking, you could be arrested as the driver of record. If you can, ask someone trustworthy about the local law, both about the law and the likely attitude of law enforcement (an acquaintance was robbed in Greece and told not to bother reporting it because the police literally wouldn't make a report. They did anyway, only to watch as the officer pretended to write notes and then tossed the paper into the garbage later. I've heard stories like this for years).

If you make a report, be as detailed as possible, but only accuse a specific person if you are absolutely and entirely sure it was them. Do not, under any circumstances, make assumptions about the identity of the perpetrator. There are strict laws about defamation that you could violate, making you a criminal. It might help to remember that you aren't making a report in hopes that the criminal will be caught, but because you'll need it to make an insurance claim later.

If you were robbed, the next step is to try to prevent future issues. Report stolen credit cards to the issuers and contact the local branch of your country's consulate about your passport. In some places, it is illegal to be without your passport, never mind needing it to get home again; replacing your passport is imperative. Use the remote wipe feature to secure your phone. Doing so prevents the crook from accessing your personal information, including saved passwords and banking login details. If medications are stolen, go to the nearest medical center to start the process of getting replacements. When doing so, remember that not all medication available over the counter or by prescription in your home country is available, or even legal, in other countries. Don't forget to cancel your rental car (it's illegal to drive without a license) if necessary.

Contact a friend or loved one to send cash to tide you over until new cards arrive.

Almost anywhere in the world, medical attention will cost you money out of pocket, even if you have traveler's insurance (travel insurance providers often have worldwide twenty-four-hour phone numbers to contact in case of trouble. Use them to find out what care you are entitled to receive).

Specific Scams

There are several scams specifically targeting travelers. Here are the most common, but I recommend you research this before traveling to check on what's new and happening in the world of scams.

- **Taxi:** Every city and airport has some variation where taxi drivers rig their meters, add fees that aren't on the meter (or listed), or say that the meter is broken. People pose as taxi drivers in many places when they are not licensed or qualified. Another scam is when they take you to establishments that pay them a commission rather than where you asked to go. Avoid this situation by only using official taxi drivers and always note their names and cab number (there is a place to report them).

- **Overcharging:** While this often happens with taxis, it can happen anywhere. You'll be in the middle of a tour or ride, and the driver will lock the doors or stop in the middle of nowhere and charge an additional fee. Frustrating and scary. If they are legitimate drivers or tour operators, you can report them, but you'll still have to pay the fee. You can avoid this in many cases by negotiating the service cost before you get into the vehicle and knowing how much it should cost (the internet is your friend for this type of research). That $30 hour-long boat ride in Thailand may sound like a deal, but it's usually only $15.
- **Skimming**: You go to use the ATM, and a helpful person will offer to help you. Instead, they'll "skim" your card's data. A variation is when an employee of an establishment skims the card you use to pay your bill. In both cases, the solution is not to let anyone near you when using an ATM and not let your card out of sight when using it.
- **Damaged property, including car or bike rentals:** You rent a scooter and have a great day tooling around, but when you return it, the owner charges you extra fees because it's been damaged. A variation is that the owner pays someone to do (minor) damage. Combat this by taking clear pictures before taking the vehicle away, ensuring the owner knows you are doing it. If they claim damage, have them prove it wasn't in your pictures.
- **Fake official:** A person in uniform asks for your ID or other official documents, then refuses to return them until you pay a fee. This is tricky because we rarely recognize whether someone in uniform is legitimate on foreign soil. If the situation is outside an official area (like a train station or airport), ask to accompany the officer to the nearest police station instead of handing over your documents. You might also ask the people around you for

assistance, "Did this person check your documents? Are they okay?" A variation of this has the fake official checking your ticket and telling you that you are in the wrong compartment. They'll offer to correct it for the difference in the ticket price. The best way to avoid this scam is to have done your research, so you know you are in the right place. Asking for help from others can also help.

The best defense against all scams is to be vigilant. Scammers, like many criminals, are looking for easy targets, the people who aren't paying attention or act gullible. If you question what's going on or fail to give in right away, they will likely give up and move on. Having lived in cities much of my life, I usually know when someone has targeted us. Making eye contact and shaking my head "no" when they head my way is usually more than enough to keep them away.

The second-best defense is remembering that if it sounds too good to be true, it almost always has something wrong.

"Just In Case" Ideas

Being prepared to have something stolen from you is not an attitude I enjoy recommending, but you can do a few (non-magical) things before you leave on your journey.

- Back up everything on your electronic devices. Do you want to lose all the photos on your phone forever? Files on your laptop? Some of us aren't backing everything up to the cloud all the time and need to be more vigilant before we travel.
- Make photocopies of all essential documents and items before you leave. Passports, credit cards (especially the back with their crucial phone numbers), and identification documents. This includes prescriptions for medications or other assistive devices (i.e., glasses). I used to make paper copies that I would tuck into a side pocket of my suitcase; now I have images and PDF files saved to various places online that I can get to, even in an internet café.

- Don't keep everything of value in one place. Share cards between multiple travelers, tuck cash into odd places in your luggage, keep a card for emergency use in a place other than your wallet, and use the room's safe if there is one.
- Consider what you would do if someone accessed your account data, which is becoming increasingly likely as we switch to oh-so-easily-stealable laptops that hold all that information. Then decide how you'll address this issue. I switch my behavior and start erasing my browser history every time I open a browser (it's a simple change in my settings at the start of a trip). My husband and I also share access to a password management service.

Chapter Seven

Specific Spells and Charms

As you dive into this chapter, please remember that these are starting points for creating versions of your own. See them as templates, not directives. If you haven't yet, please read Chapter Two: Correspondences so you know how and why the symbols I use were chosen and how you can modify them to fit your perspective. If the color of a candle I use doesn't make sense to you, then certainly use the color that does make sense. These have been tested to my satisfaction, and you could do worse than at least trying one once if you aren't sure; maybe we're in tune enough with each other that they'll work "straight out of the box," so to speak.

Any one of these might have an invocation to a travel-focused deity added or the casting of a formal circle. If you must work your magic quickly (which happens way too often on our journeys!), then doing the stripped-down outlines will be enough.

A Traveler's Spell

Malachite is one of my all-time favorite stones; it's so versatile.

You will need:

- Malachite, enough for you and each piece of luggage
- Your luggage

Stand in front of your luggage with the malachite in your dominant hand. Take three breaths and center yourself. Say out loud:

"My bag(s) always come to me.
As I will, so mote it be!"

Place one of the stones in each bag and one in your pocket (or purse).

Airplane Spell

You can substitute a drawing of an airplane for the toy in this delightful spell. It's beneficial when your journey involves many flights.

You will need:

- A toy airplane
- Sharp knife
- 1 tbsp of anise essential oil
- 1 cup clover
- 1 cup of uncooked rice

Take three breaths and center yourself. Take your toy airplane and carve a pentagram on any part of it while visualizing yourself flying safely and protected. Anoint the airplane with anise oil. Take another three deep breaths and center yourself comfortably in a chair. Hold the plane in your two hands. Feel the breath within your body mix with the air surrounding you and the plane.

When it feels right, gently blow air from your mouth and lift the plane using both hands. See the plane doing this as if taking off from the airport. Breathing steadily, push the plane slowly away. You may wish to turn the plane this way and that for a bit, following its presumed flight path, breathing steadily and gently, holding the plane securely upright and level. When you are finished, bring the plane gently back in for a landing, settling in your lap.

Place the plane on your altar, surround it with rice and clover, and leave for at least one whole night before departing. Leave the plane on your altar while you travel.

Attract Travel into Your Life

I went on my first international trip at the ripe age of forty, years after everyone else I knew. This spell helped manifest that journey.

You will need:

- A small fan
- A small feather, preferably light-colored
- Mint, dried
- A small dish

Place the mint into the dish. Take three breaths and center yourself. Say aloud: "I want to travel. For me, travel means..." then describe why you want to travel and what you think it will bring into your life. When you are finished describing travel, lean over the bowl of mint and inhale the scent. While inhaling, visualize the scents, scenery, and experiences of the travel you desire.

Toss the feather into the air and use the fan to keep the feather airborne. Imagine the feather is you, moving to different places in the world. Allow the feather to come to rest in the mint. Take a few more breaths of the minty aroma. Each day, for at least three days, inhale the scent of the mint and visualize your travels.

Braid Charm

An extension of knot magic, braiding ribbons are often used for protection spells. This charm is an unobtrusive way of promoting safety and protection during travel.

You will need:

- Three equal lengths of ribbon or embroidery thread
    - Dark blue for clarity
    - Yellow for communication and travel
    - Brown for safety and endurance
- Large safety pin

Take three breaths and center yourself. Start by pinning the three ribbons together at the top, then braid. As you braid, say out loud:

"[Name of deity], I invoke Thee
Cords in hand, numbering three.
I braid these strands together into one
Power combined, not to be undone.
Wherever I travel, over stone or sea
I ask Thee [Name] to protect me."

As you come to the end of the braid, unhook it from the safety pin and tie a knot into all six strands (three at the top, three at the bottom), forming a loop. You will carry this braid with you as you travel.

An alternative is to make several braids, one for carrying and one for each piece of luggage. In this case, as you come to the end of the weaving, unhook it from the pin and wrap it around the handle of your luggage (or tie it to a zipper closure).

This charm can easily be customized by adding beads or travel and protection-themed charms to the end of the braid.

Carnelian Charm for Clear Communication

Sometimes we need extra eloquence to smooth out a snarled situation during our travels. Perhaps the flight time was changed, your connection plans need to be fixed, and you need someone to make it right.

This charm uses carnelian and the power of Mercury to aid in being heard and appearing charming and eloquent (as a bonus, if you are traveling for business, this charm aids in public speaking and enhances self-confidence).

You will need:

- Small piece of carnelian
- Benzoin incense (or another incense sacred to Mercury)

Take three breaths and center yourself. Light the incense and move the carnelian through the smoke three times, saying out loud:

"I call to Thee, Eloquent God Mercury
The best one to help me, I know with certainty.
Aid me in finding words of persuasion and argument
In clearing away all impediments.
Mercury, O Quick-Witted one, empower this stone
With all Your eloquence, keenly honed.
With thanks, giving honor, I bow to Thee (bow)
Master of Travel, over stone and sea!"

Place the stone under your pillow and sleep with it, paying particular attention to your dreams (this is not, strictly speaking, necessary. If you don't have time, don't fret and go on to the next part). Carry the stone with you when trying to unsnarl the issue. If you get stuck for words, tongue-tied, or nervous, touch the stone and feel Mercury's power assisting you in finding the right words to say.

Charm Bag to Avert Anxiety

Traveling is often full of worry. This bag accesses the power of affirmation to create a personal charm that tends to kick out anxiety. If you keep everything small for this charm, it's easier to carry the bag to touch it when you need reassurance or soothing.

You will need:

- A small bag
- A piece of paper
- Something to write with
- A piece of amethyst
- Chamomile and lavender, dried

An affirmation is a concise statement in the present tense that can strengthen self-worth. They are an excellent tool to help counter the feelings of panic, stress, and self-doubt most of us experience when anxious. An example of an anxiety-specific affirmation might be, "I am calm," "I am capable," or even, "I am safe and in control." Create the phrase that suits you and your situation best.

Take three breaths and center yourself. Write the affirmation on the paper and roll it up to fit in the bag. Add the herbs and amethyst. Hold the bag in your dominant hand and breathe calmly for several minutes, focusing on your intent.

Carry the bag with you and connect with its soothing, strengthening power when needed.

Charm for Safe Travels

This charm wards the traveler against three common dangers: getting stranded, physical harm, and theft. The charm item is best if it is small and easy to carry. I use a compass charm initially intended for a bracelet, but something you might hang from the rearview mirror or a piece of jewelry to wear when you travel would also work well.

You will need:

- An item to charm
- Black salt to ward against theft
- Bay leaf
- Chamomile
- Two small candles (tea lights work nicely)
- Small bowl

Set the two candles on a flat surface at least a foot apart, the bowl between them. Light the candles. Take three breaths and center yourself. Pour the black salt into the bowl, saying aloud:

"I am guarded against thieves."

Place the bay leaf into the bowl, saying aloud:

"I am protected from all harm."

Sprinkle the chamomile into the bowl, saying aloud:

"My footsteps are led by luck."

Set your charm into the bowl on top of the herbs. Move the bowl to the left with your dominant hand until it nearly touches the candle. Slowly slide the bowl to the right so it "travels" to the other candle and say the first line of the incantation below. Slide it back to the left and recite the second line, then right again as you say the third line. For the final line of the incantation, center the bowl between the candles again.

"From here to there, does safety follow (slide bowl to the right)
There and back, it follows still (slide bowl to the left)
Out again my steps may lead me (slide bowl to the right again)
And safely so, as is my will (move bowl to center)."

Allow the candles to burn themselves out.

Remove the item from the bowl and take it when traveling. Keep the herbs and salt in the bowl. Before leaving on your trip, sprinkle a small handful outside your doorstep and walk over it as you leave (be careful not to get the salt onto the dirt as it will kill it—pretty much the opposite of what Witchcraft is about).

Destination Divination

While I don't use this divination often, it's been enormously valuable when I have.[36]

You will need:

- A Tarot deck
- A map or images of your trip destinations

Once you have all your destinations planned for your trip, mark them on a map (alternatively, gather images of your destinations).

Shuffle your Tarot deck and ask, "What energy do I need to get the most out of or at this destination?" Do this for each place you plan to visit. Write down what card you pull for the different places and journal your thoughts about it for a few minutes (if you're using printed images, write on the back of the page).

---

36 The time we ignored the information was a spectacular learning opportunity.

Keep these notes with you as you go from place to place. Stay open to how the cards' energy is reflected in everything you experience in different places.

Fast Sigil Charm for Protection

I created this charm on a paper napkin while sitting in a food court before flying to a city with a very...shall we say, *sketchy* vibe. Scammers and the like targeted people around me while I was there, ignoring me throughout.

You will need:

- Paper
- Pencil
- Thread

Set aside time when you can be private. Take three breaths and center yourself. Decide what protection means and write it succinctly in the present tense (for more on creating sigils, see Chapter Four)

On a different piece of paper, write the word PROTECTION. Strike out repeating letters and all vowels (PRTCN). Then, layer those letters in a pattern you find pleasing. While doing so, strongly feel that you are protected (take your time with this, enjoy yourself).

When finished, recreate your sigil on a clean piece of paper. Fold the paper at least three times and as many as nine. Wrap the paper in the thread while chanting:

"Protection, protection, I carry with me.
As I will, so mote it be!"

Keep the charm with you on your journey.

This charm doesn't last very long as the paper is fragile. You can make it more permanent by etching the sigil on wood or metal. If you do so, don't wrap the charm as you chant; hold it in your dominant hand. Use a cord to hang the charm or tie it to your purse or luggage.

Ginger Safe Travel Spell

Best performed on a Thursday, this spell helps keep journeys smooth and free from mishaps. It's excellent when you travel a lot as it only needs to be renewed every six months.

You will need:

- Ginger root, shaped as much like a human as possible (you can carve or draw on it to increase the likeness)
- Three yellow ribbons
- Small wooden box

Take three breaths and center yourself.

Decorate the figure with yellow ribbons tied in three places. The choice of where is up to you, but *do not* tie anything around the neck. You might use places like the wrists, legs, midsection, or arms. As you tie a knot in each ribbon, wish for positive luck and chant the following:

"In all the journeys of my life,
protect and keep me safe from strife."

Place the figure in the wooden box, seal the lid, and keep it in a safe, dry place. Make contact with the figure before each significant journey.

Hands of Deity Visualization

For years I have done a specific visualization during take-off and landing, the most dangerous times in any flight.

As the plane taxis down the tarmac, I close my eyes, tuck my head back, and mentally open my arms wide. I call out to a deity (for me specifically, it is Mercury, but any deity you feel offers protection is a good choice). I see the deity standing behind the plane, holding it in Its hands. As we pick up speed, I ask that this be a good, safe flight and see Them lifting the plane up and off the ground. They lift the plane into the air, releasing it at cruising altitude. As the flight finishes, I envision the reverse, with Them cradling the plane in their palms, gently lowering it to the tarmac, and safely to the gate. I do not use specific words, but I do ask politely and thank profusely when the flight is thoroughly grounded.

Jupiter Candle Spell

This spell calls upon the energy of the planet Jupiter, which rules travel. It's best done on a Thursday or the day before you travel. You can roll the

You will need:

- A short candle
- Something sharp to carve the candle
- Oil
- A cloth to wipe your hands
- Rosemary, dried
- A piece of rose quartz

Carve the glyph for Jupiter into the candle. Anoint the candle with the oil and roll in the rosemary (Note: don't use too much as it can make the candle burn too hot for safety). Place the candle into a fireproof dish and lay the rose quartz in front.

Take three breaths and center yourself. Light the candle and give the flame time to burn intensely. Gaze into the flame, breathing the scent of rosemary. When you feel the time is right, chant:

"By the light of Jupiter and its many moons
My travels magnificent, under his boon.
The trip kept secure, for all accompanying me
As I will, so mote it be!"

Let the candle burn out if possible. Take the rose quartz with you on your journey.

Knot Ladder Travel Spell

Knot magic, or "Witch's ladders," is old magic. This particular version is from my Book of Shadows, added there sometime in 2003.

You will only need a length of bright blue ribbon.

Take three breaths and center yourself. Using a bright blue cord or ribbon, tie seven knots. With each knot, say the following:

"Knot of one, my spell's begun.
Knot of two, my destination is true.
Knot of three, my route I see.
Knot of four, my safety is sure.
Knot of five, I safely drive.
Knot of six, my spell is fixed.
Knot of seven, the power wakens."

You might hang the knotted cord from your rear-view mirror while driving or keep it in the glove compartment. Renew quarterly.

Luggage Protection Stone Pouch

I always check my bags, tucking a bit of protection into the side pocket (I have never lost a bag; the worst was a day's delay).

You will need:

- Small bag
- Amber
- Moonstone
- Quartz

Hold the stones in your dominant hand. Take three breaths and center yourself. Say aloud:

"All is safe while I am away
Enjoying a perfect holiday.

Luggage, take care and meet me there
Secure and safe from wear"

Place the stones into the bag, then tuck the bag into the suitcase. Keep them there through the trip. Remove when you are finished traveling and renew the spell with each trip.

Once you feel the bag is charged, take it to your vehicle. Here you have two options:

1. Leave it where it won't be noticed (or removed).
2. Hang it from your rearview mirror. Doing this allows sunlight to feed more energy into your spell, but if it distracts you, don't do this (that would defeat the purpose).

Use three knots to tie the bag closed (or to the mirror) while saying aloud:

"With each knot, I bind this spell
Safety, protection, all is well
Sheltered and shielded, this vehicle shall be
Three times three, so mote it be!"

Renew the pouch occasionally. If you can't smell it anymore, that's a sign it's out of power and needs renewing.

Mercury Charm Bag

Working with Mercury is an excellent way to ensure safe and smooth travel. This bag brings His energy to your journey.

You will need:

- Flannel cloth in green or blue (any natural cloth will do, but the softness of flannel makes this cozy)
- Penny
- Symbol of how you will primarily travel: plane, car, boat, etc.
- Paper

- Writing instrument, ideally using green or blue ink
- Essential oil (geranium or lemon are good)
- Blue thread

Take three breaths and center yourself. On the paper, write out:

"Fleet-footed Mercury,
Smooth my travel, make it steady,
Without delays.
Quick-witted Mercury,
Watch over me.
Keep me safe when far from home,
Returning carefree."

Anoint the parchment with the oil and place it on the cloth. Add the penny and travel symbol. Wrap the cloth up and use the thread to hold it together. Carry the bag with you when you travel.

MOONSTONE TRAVEL SPELL, VERSION ONE

While best cast under the full moon, the stone can be charged anytime you have a trip coming up.

You will need:

- Moonstone
- White candle

Place the candle on a flat surface. Take three breaths and center yourself. Hold the moonstone in your dominant hand. Connect to the moon's energy and feel it flow into you and the stone. When it feels fully charged, set the stone down by a window and cast say aloud:

"As I travel far away
I call protection throughout the day
With this stone charged in the moonlight
I call protection throughout the night

As I travel far and near
Bring me safely right back here"

Repeat three times, then light the candle. Allow them to burn out. Put the stone in your luggage for your journey.

MOONSTONE TRAVEL SPELL, VERSION TWO

This spell is more elaborate than the others I've shared. Ideally, you'll be able to do it in an evening when the Moon is full (or waxing near its peak) on a Monday, and you'll be able to burn a lunar-oriented incense, such as jasmine.

You will need:

- A photo of your destination, your travel itinerary, or your airline tickets
- Four moonstones (you can use more, but not fewer)
- A small white candle (tea or votive size is ideal)

Set the candle on a flat surface. Take three breaths and center yourself, then light the candle. Place your paperwork, tickets, or itinerary on one side of the candle and place the stones equidistant around the holder.

Place another stone on the travel item(s) and hold your hands over the pile. Say out loud:

"Mercury, patron of travelers, watch over me
Whether I travel in the air, on land, or sea.
Charge this stone with your power
Here and now in this hour.
In my pocket, this stone will I tuck
To ensure a safe journey and bring good luck."

Allow the candle to burn out on its own. Keep the moonstone on the documents until you are ready to travel, then take the stone on top of them with you.

If you perform this outside, move your candle and all the items indoors to let the candle safely finish burning. Never leave your candles unattended.

Quick Car Protection Chant

This is the fastest way to protect you and your vehicle, ideal for when you rent a car. With energy and intention in place, walk around the vehicle three times, chanting:

"As I travel near and far
I call on Spirit to protect this car."

On the front and back of the car, draw a rune of protection (Eolh/ Algiz or Raido) with your finger.

Algiz *Raido*

Travel-Specific Runes

Rosemary Luggage Protection

I always check my bags, and rosemary is easy to find.
You will need:

- Sprig of rosemary
- Purple ribbon

Take three breaths and center yourself. Place the rosemary inside your case, then trace a pentagram (star) over each zipper clasp or lock.

Weave the ribbon securely around the handle of your case while saying out loud:

"Protected is this suitcase of mine
It will always return safely, in good time."

A variation of this is to use a brightly colored or patterned luggage tag instead of a ribbon. Tuck a bit of rosemary into the holder (behind the card with your name and address) and say the charm while clasping it to your suitcase.[37]

Safe Travels Sachet, Version One

This sachet is perfect for your carry-on, checked bag, or car.

You will need:

- Yellow candle
- Orange zest
- Bay leaves
- Lavender
- Blue thread
- Salt (sea salt is best, but any kind will do)
- Sage, dried
- Small bag

Place the candle on a flat surface. Take three breaths and center yourself. While visualizing yourself (and your loved ones) safe and secure during your travels, add the above items to the bag, contemplating the protective qualities of each as you do so. Tie it off with the blue string.

Take a few moments to hold the bag in your dominant hand and charge it with protective energy, visualizing your vehicle surrounded by a bubble (I like to use blue for the bubble). Feel the energy tingling in your palms and passing into the bag and its contents.

37 Don't forget to change the destination; this is the address they use to deliver late bags.

Let the bag sit in the candle's light until it burns out.

You can place the bag under the driver's seat of your car or keep it in your luggage while you travel. If in your car, recharge every few months for maximum effectiveness; otherwise, renew with each journey.

Safe Travels Sachet, Version Two

This sachet is perfect for keeping in your carry-on, checked bag, or car.

You will need:

- Yellow candle
- Bag made of black or yellow fabric
- Three herbs from this list: Basil, cedar, comfrey, pennyroyal, cinquefoil, or lavender
- One or more stones from this list: Malachite, amethyst, citrine, or angelite

Place the candle on a flat surface. Take three breaths and center yourself. While visualizing yourself safe and secure during your travels, add the above items to the bag, contemplating the protective qualities of each as you do so.

Take a few moments to hold the bag in your dominant hand and charge it with protective energy, visualizing your vehicle surrounded by a bubble. Feel the energy tingling in your palms and passing into the bag and its contents.

You can place the bag under the driver's seat of your car or keep it in your luggage while you travel. If in your car, recharge every few months for maximum effectiveness; otherwise, renew with each journey.

Safe Travel Bottle

This bottle stays safe at home so that you travel and return safely (for instructions on how to create a sigil, see Chapter Four).

Ideally, this would be done when the Moon is waxing or full.

You will need:

- Yellow candle
- Small bottle with a stopper
- Basil
- Sage
- Bay leaf
- Lavender
- Chamomile
- Sigil for safe travel

Place the candle in the center of a flat surface and lay the travel items around it in a rough circle.

Take three breaths and center yourself. Light the yellow candle and contemplate your intentions for a moment. Begin layering the herbs in the bottle in the order listed above, contemplating the properties of each one as you do so. Visualize yourself having a safe and happy trip. When the bottle is full, burn the sigil to activate it and place the ashes into the bottle on top of the other ingredients. Put in the stopper and seal the bottle with wax from the candle. Leave to charge in the moonlight overnight.

Safe Travel Spell

Rowan Moonstone gave me the bones of this spell when I told her I was writing this book. Erin Angel and Gracie Weber created the original.

You will need:

- Four candles, two white, one purple, and one in the color you feel best represents the personality of the person traveling (in the image below, I used blue)
- Vegetable oil with three drops of sandalwood essential oil added
- Sandalwood incense
- Cloth for wiping your hands

Take three breaths and center yourself. Using the needle, inscribe the traveler's name on the "personality" candle. Using the scented vegetable oil, anoint all candles, then roll them in powdered sandalwood (wipe your hands).

Place the personality candle in the center of your altar (or other flat space where you can leave this working undisturbed), with a white candle on the left, the purple candle on the right, and the second white candle in front of the first white one. Finally, place the incense in front of the purple candle. It will look like this:

White Candle	Personality Candle	Purple Candle
White Candle		Incense

Spell Candle Layout

Light the candles, starting with the white candles, then the personality candle, and ending with the purple candle. Then light the incense. Contemplate the candles and breathe the incense for a bit. Visualize the journey as thoroughly as possible, ending with the traveler returning home safe and happy.

When you feel ready, chant:

"Hail, Mother of the World
Nanna, Isis, Astarte, Selena
Holy Sin (pronounced Sheen).
See me, look upon me
See me, look upon me
See me, look upon me.
Protect me and my people tonight
Send your white light around me.
Send your protective light around [name]
That they may be protected as they travel
And as they dream.
Send only good and lucid energies their way.
Thank you
Thank you
Thank you."

Safe Travel Spell Jar

Spell jars don't come with you on the journey but remain at home. This version acts as a touchstone for you to return safely.

You will need:

- A small jar that has a secure lid or stopper
- Sea salt (although any salt will do)
- Eggshells
- Orange peel, dried
- Tiger's eye
- Lavender and mint, dried

Take three breaths and center yourself. Spend time looking at your ingredients and creating a clear intention that your journey will be safe and secure.

Slowly add the ingredients to the jar, thinking about why each one is a part of the spell. Add the ingredients in the order listed above. Seal the jar when you are finished.[38]

Spell for Positive Outlook

This spell enhances the energy of travel, creating a positive outlook throughout your journey (it's particularly useful if you tire of being on the go every day).

You will need:

- Four candles, one each in red, green, yellow, and blue (alternatively, use white candles)
- One or two herbs
- A square of blue cloth
- Incense (use anything that smells exotic)
- Feather

38 Since this is a spell you didn't create, I suggest you research the ingredients using Chapter Two: Correspondences.

- A map on which your travel path is outlined
- Red thread

Ideally, this spell is created on a full moon or a Monday.

Position your map in the center of the circle, and place the four candles at the four quarters, East, South, West, and North. Take three breaths and center yourself. Light the candles and the incense, and chant this verse three times:

"Fire, Air, Water, and Earth,
I ask your protection, all it's worth.
Red, green, yellow, blue:
Take my dreams and make them true."

Fold the herbs inside the map and wrap them in the cloth. Tie the bundle with the red thread and knot the feather onto the bundle. Carry in your luggage.

Spell for Safe Return

Another spell given to me by Rowan Moonstone for this book, originally from Erin Angel and Gracie Weber.

You will need:

- Four candles, two white, one purple, and one in the color you feel best represents the personality of the person traveling (in the image, I used blue)
- Vegetable oil
- Powdered sandalwood
- Sandalwood incense
- Cloth handkerchief (for travel charm)
- Tapestry needle (or other sharp, fine-pointed tool, like an awl)
- Cloth for wiping your hands

Take three breaths and center yourself. Using the needle, inscribe the traveler's name on the "personality" candle. Using the vegetable oil, anoint all candles, then roll them in powdered sandalwood (wipe your hands).

Place the personality candle in the center of your altar (or other flat space where you can leave this working undisturbed) with one white candle on the left, the purple candle on the right, and the second white candle in front of the first one. Finally, place the incense in front of the purple candle. It will look like this:

White Candle	Personality Candle	Purple Candle
White Candle		Incense

Spell Candle Layout

Light the two white candles, the personality candle, the purple candle, and the incense in that order. Contemplate the candles and breathe the incense for a bit. Visualize the journey as thoroughly as possible, ending with the traveler returning home safe and happy.

When you feel ready, chant:

"Mother of the World arise
Watch over [me/us] with keen eyes.
As [I/we] travel, shed Your light
Keep [me/us] safe both day and night.
Watch over [my/our] belongings, please,
Grant [my/our] trip be filled with peace.
Protect [me/us] for [I am/we are] Your own
Guide [me/us] safely back home."

Let the candles burn down completely. Collect the burned wicks or left-over wax, if there is any, in a cloth handkerchief. Tie the upper right-hand and lower left-hand corners together, then the lower right-hand and upper left-hand corners together to secure. Carry the handkerchief on the journey, or hold it until the traveler returns before disposing of properly.

Successful Travel Bath Spell

Sadly, this two-part bathing spell won't work in a shower.

You will need:

- Four tealights
- Yellow candle
- A few drops of protective essential oil, such as sandalwood or vetiver

Place the tealights safely at the four corners of the bathtub, ideally aligning with the four directions. Draw yourself a bath and add the essential oil to the bathwater. Light the yellow candle.

Get in the water and visualize all your cares being washed away. When it feels right, bring your attention to the upcoming journey. Focus on how much you will enjoy the journey.

When it feels right, look at the yellow candle and ask, using your own words, for guidance and assistance in being open to opportunities to enjoy the upcoming new experiences. Ask that you find the people you need to meet for the best experience.

Gently extinguish the candles when you have finished your bath.

When you return home from your journey, draw another bath (no essential oils this time). Relight the candles. After getting into the bath, spend some time remembering the best moments of the journey. Using your own words, say thank you.

Successful Travel Shower Spell

You will need:

- Yellow candle
- Few drops of protective essential oil, such as sandalwood or vetiver

Lightly trace the essential oil over the yellow candle, thinking about the upcoming journey. Light the yellow candle and set it into a heat-safe container.

As you step into the shower, imagine the water cleansing and purifying you, washing away any negativity or stagnant energy. Feel the water's rejuvenating and revitalizing power. As the water flows over you, focus on how much you will enjoy the coming journey. Using your own words, ask for guidance and assistance in being open to opportunities to enjoy the new experiences. Ask that you find the people you need to meet for the best experience.

When you exit the shower, gently extinguish the candle and keep it in a safe place.

When you return home from your journey, take another shower, relight the yellow candle. Get into the shower and spend some time remembering the best moments of the journey. Using your own words, say thank you.

Tarot Card Spell

While I only carry Tarot cards with me when I travel to a conference, this spell gives me their protection on any journey.

You will need:

- The Six of Swords, The Fool, and Three of Cups Tarot cards
- Three stones to which you feel a strong connection

Take three breaths and center yourself. Set out the Six of Swords, The Fool, and the Three of Cups cards from your favorite Tarot deck in front of you, going from left to right.

Place the first of three stones you feel strongly connected to on the Six of Swords card, saying:

"For safe travel."

Place the second stone on The Fool, saying:

"For a mind and heart open to adventure."

Place the third stone on the Three of Cups, saying:

"For a celebratory homecoming."

Leave the spread to charge overnight in the moonlight. The following day, cleanse the cards and return them to the pack. Place the stones in the bag and take the bag with you on your trip.

Travel Charm Bag

This is a charm bag you use as an offering, so I don't recommend it if you are going on a long journey with multiple stops. However, it is perfect for a place you plan to return to several times.

You will need:

- A small bag you can easily tuck into a pocket or purse
- Penny
- A personal item, such as hair or a photograph
- Malachite
- Tiger's eye
- Sage
- Rosemary

Fill the bag with the items, placing each one in the bag with intention and a verbal statement (i.e., "This penny is my offering to the spirits of the place. This stone [property of the stone]."[39]

Travel safely, and when you arrive, find an appropriate place to leave it (a fountain, a donation box, a child's piggy bank, etc.) as an offering.

Travel Sachet

This sachet takes time, so start well before you think you'll use it. The sachet can be brought with you on a journey or kept in your car.

You will need:

39 See Chapter Two: Correspondences for specific information about each item chosen.

- A paper bag big enough to hold the herbs
- Comfrey, mint, and rosemary, all fresh
- Lemon (peel)
- A cloth bag of natural fiber (like cotton, hemp, or linen)
- Thread (I prefer blue, but that isn't a rule)

Take three breaths and center yourself. Take the herbs and use the thread to tie them together in a long bundle. Place the bound herbs into the paper bag with the lemon peel, then tie the opening closed around them, leaving a length of thread outside. Use the thread to hang the bag and herbs in a high, dry location.

When the herbs have completely dried, strip the leaves from the stems back into the bag with the dried peel. Pour the mix into the cloth bag while chanting:

"By the light of stars, Sun, and Moon
My journey safe, by your boon.
The trip secure, for all accompanying me
As I will, so mote it be!"

Travel Safely Spell

Who doesn't need a little extra protection when traveling?

You will need:

- Candle (I like bright blue)
- Fresh mint leaves (you can substitute a piece of mint candy)
- Between three and seven travel-specific items (for a beach vacation, this might be your sunglasses, bathing suit, and passport)
- A piece of quartz crystal

Place the candle in the center of a flat surface and lay the travel items around it in a rough circle.

Take three breaths and center yourself. Light the candle and hold the crystal in your dominant hand. Visualize your journey. Imagine the steps of the actual trip, ending with your safe arrival at the destination. See everything going smoothly and you feeling peaceful and calm. While doing this, program the crystal with this safe, smooth journey energy.

When you feel ready, quietly but with feeling, chant:

"Stone so clear, like sky and sea
On my journey, protect me.
Let no harm come near
Keep me safe from injury and fear.
Let me reach my destination
In good health, ready for relaxation
As I spread my wings and soar,
From road to road and shore to shore."

Eat one of the pieces of mint and sprinkle the remaining leaves around the items. When ready, snuff the candle and get a good night's rest. During your journey, carry the stone in a pocket and feel confident that your journey is going smoothly. If anything worries you, hold the crystal in your receptive hand and ask for a boost to your protection.

Travel Talisman

This is excellent for either a regular commute or a one-time journey.

You will need:

- A drawstring bag in red or white
- A combination of the following herbs: rose petals, lilac, foxglove, devil's shoestring, wormwood, orris root, and witch hazel
- Moonstone or turquoise

Add the herbs to the bag, contemplating the energy of each and what it will bring you as you travel. Place the stone in the bag with the same knowledge. Visualize a safe and pleasant journey and joyful return home as you tie the pouch closed, making five knots.

With each knot, chant:

"As I wander, as I roam,
Far away or close to home;
Keep me safe along the way,
Guard my journey night and day."

Keep the bundle in your car or carry it during the journey.

Travel-by-Water Talisman

This talisman is inspired by one Amber K. created years ago.

You will need:

- Small silver or blue cloth bag
- Pen with silver or blue ink
- Paper
- A tiny bit of cork
- Small shell
- A tiny dolphin or an image of a dolphin

At the full moon, assemble the items on your altar and cast a circle. Use the pen to draw symbols of Venus and Neptune on the paper. Take three breaths and center yourself. Holding your hands over the items, chant:

"Venus and Neptune, blessed be
Protect your child while on the sea.
As the dolphin happily roams
I will come safely home.
Protect your child on the sea.
Venus, Neptune, blessed be!"

Repeat the chant three times as you place the items in the bag.

Vehicle Protection Sachet Spell

Most of us travel a lot in our car. Maybe it's just around town or across the city, but extra protection is always good to keep us safe.

You will need:

- A small bag or a piece of cloth and a ribbon
- Sage (dried)
- Rosemary (dried)
- Pinch of salt (coarse/kosher is best)
- Three small pieces of dragon's blood (use a hefty pinch if powdered)
- Three cat whiskers[40]
- A small piece of amethyst

Take three breaths and center yourself. While visualizing yourself (and your loved ones) safe and secure in your vehicle, add the above items to the charm bag, contemplating the protective qualities of each as you do so. Take a few moments to hold the bag in your dominant hand and charge it with protective energy, visualizing your vehicle surrounded by a bubble (I like blue for the bubble). Feel the energy tingling in your palms and passing into the bag and its contents.

40 I really hope I don't have to tell you to not pull out your cat's whiskers. My cats left me whiskers all the time, which I collected in a jar. If you don't have a cat, or your cat doesn't leave you whiskers, skip this item and replace it with something that resonates with you. You might use a small bird feather or a pretty seashell.

Chapter Eight

Travel is a State of Mind

Travel is wonderful, but it's not for everyone. I can't put it any plainer than that.

In late 2021, my husband and I sold almost everything we owned and moved to Portugal. Here, we are creating a truly magnificent life with a community of people and a far better quality of life than we previously had in the States. From where we are, travel is simple and inexpensive. We can take one of several buses a day to Paris for less than $100, or to Madrid for roughly half of that. The country itself has excellent train and bus service, and a flight to anywhere in the EU runs out of the local-ish airport forty-five minutes away. Most EU countries have excellent and inexpensive public transportation. *Bottom line:* Travel is made easy and affordable here.

This level of access and affordability is not typical in the United States.

Many people think travel is luxury, a vision supported by online accounts asking provocative questions like: "Quiet Luxury vs. Luxury Porn—Which luxury travel style do you prefer?" ("Quiet Luxury" is apparently defined by "understated, timeless, and minimal designs" without overt branding. "Luxury Porn" is "opulent, eye-catching, and visibly high-end"; it's meant to be noticed). Both "styles" are ridiculous and miss the entire point of travel.

The point? It's different for each of us. For some travel offers enticingly new food to try, art to experience, different weather, adventurous encounters, a gateway to the unknown, or something else entirely.

I want to make it abundantly clear that when I talk about travel, I am talking about any time we leave the safety of our home environment. Whether we are going down the street for a bottle of milk, or into town for a meal, that is travel as much as a hiking trip in a National Park or month-long crawl through the Dolomites.

How to Travel Without Leaving Home

Whatever your reason for wanting to travel without leaving your home environment, there are many ways to do so.

Astrocartography

Find the place "perfect" for you according to the stars, then experience every aspect of it that you can. Read books by its authors. Find locals who post on social media and follow them. One of my favorite astrology websites, Astrodienst (as previously mentioned), has a free calculator with interpretations for the various lines and computations.

Fall Into a Good Book

Fiction can transport us to any place or time if we let it. For some of us, escaping into a book has always been an adventurous pleasure. You might visit Wonderland with Alice, Thugz Mansion with Tupac, Discworld with The Librarian, The Restaurant at the End of the Universe with Arthur, or perhaps Narnia with Lucy. Don't find the strange places you want to experience in a book? Write your own.

View a Random Street

MapCrunch (mapcrunch.com) is a fascinating place. Arriving at the website shows you a random Google Street View somewhere in the world. You can either explore that area, using the arrows to venture as far as you'd like, or click "Go!" in the top left and be transported somewhere else. On a recent visit, my first view was the Rialto water taxi stop in Venice (IT), then a highway in Santa Rosa, CA (USA), followed by a quiet street in Brazil.

Visit Exotic Wildlife

Thanks to technology, there are webcams all over the world that allow you to get close to a wide variety of wildlife, from big cats to birds and sea life. YouTube is a great source for this, just put "livestream + [any animal]" in their search bar and enjoy the content.

Create Your Own Adventure

Guided meditation can take you anywhere and offers a useful way to explore the world. I find the ones where the script has me focusing on the environment's sensations—the sound of waves at the beach, the feel of the sand under my feet, the smell of salt—especially valuable for getting me into that place instead of my apartment.

Learn a New Language

Science shows that learning a new language is one way to build mental resilience. When we learn a language, we combine novelty with practice by (for example) taking new words and grammatical constructs and exercising our brain workout. Doing so seems to protect older learners against dementia and other degenerative neurological conditions. Just trying to learn seems to improve memory, communication skills, and creativity. There are a variety of apps, including Duolingo, Dropz, and Memrise, as well as several well-known programs, like Babbel, Pimsleur, and Rosetta Stone.

Create a Vision Board

Print colorful images, charts, and maps; write out plans in detail. Put it all together on a digital or physical board and enjoy how it feels to see. You might include images of maps, exotic pottery or other crafts, or animals. There are many images to access on places like Pinterest (pinterest.com) and Creative Commons (creativecommons.org).

Virtually Visit Popular Tourist Destinations

Always wanted to see the ball drop over Times Square on New Year's Eve? The canals of Venice? Skyline is a website with a collection of very popular webcams streaming from all over the world.[41] A recent visit showed the Piazza di Spagna (Rome, Italy), Mt. Etna (Sicily, Italy), Playa del Duque (Tenerife, Spain), Anse Parnel Takamaka (Quatre Bornes, Seychelles), and too many more to list (I was distracted for hours).

Be a Tourist in Your Own Town

I grew up in San Francisco, lived in New York City, and we used to live near Seattle. We only saw popular or famous attractions when we had company, and even then, I've never been to Ellis Island. Go off-season and you'll miss the crowds and might even enjoy bargain pricing. Where you live is interesting!

Explore Areas Nearby

Growing up, we had very little extra money, and family vacations were minimally supplied camping events. We'd load up a cooler and a shopping bag with food, throw them, sleeping bags and a couple of backpacks into the trunk of the car, and drive off to a National Park somewhere in California. The only camping-specific gear we had were our sleeping bags and a camp stove (and let me tell you that cleaning soot off our kitchen dishes and pans was a major PITA). We bought firewood near where we camped and had only a tarp to put on the ground. If it rained, we went home.

41 Skyline, *Skyline Webcams,* Visoray, 2025, skylinewebcams.com/en/top-live-cams.html.

Eat Your Way Around the World

Bless his soul, Anthony Bourdain opened the world to our palates and gave us adventure aplenty in his *Parts Unknown* and *No Reservations* travel shows. He went seemingly everywhere—Iran, the Congo, Peru, China, Libya, Greece—and ate everything from street food to home-cooked feasts to *haute cuisine.* What makes this show unique is how Bourdain's incisive commentary situates the food within the richer context of a region's culture, politics, history and struggles. *Hairy Bikers* combines cooking with motorcycle-based travelogue, primarily in Britain. If you want something elevated, *Chef's Table* is a beautifully filmed and written documentary series. Each episode focuses on a world-renowned chef and their story.

Create a Staycation

Perhaps this is no longer fun after the rigors of the pandemic, but it can be a fun way to travel and relax all at once. A friend regularly does this as she has a severely compromised immune system, and she gave me some tips. First, allocate money as if you were leaving home, then—do all the things! Some ideas might include hiring a personal trainer for a daily workout. Hire a chef to cook a special meal and clean up. Find and explore all of the local museums. Eat lunch out at a new place every day. Check out the chamber of commerce and see the things they tell tourists.

Utilize TV Shows

Rick Steves and Samantha Brown are popular for a good reason: their shows are fun and informative. But there are more to enjoy:

- *Expedition Unknown*: Josh Gates uses his background in archaeology to investigate unsolved mysteries, lost cities, and buried treasure around the world

- *Planet Earth*: This much-awarded series from the BBC offers breathtaking episodes featuring a different biome or habitat. Viewers are taken from the Arctic and Antarctica to the depths of the oceans.
- *Long Way Round*: Two actors (Ewan McGregor and Charley Boorman) ride east from London to New York, a route that takes them through Europe, Asia, and Alaska, and then down to the contiguous United States, usually off-road (if you like this, you might enjoy their sequel, *Long Way Down*).

Join a Virtual Travel Experience

Local guides take visitors on a live, interactive, personal tour using the latest Mobile Augmented or Virtual Reality technologies (I'm sort of extra fascinated by this). YouGo.World offers programs specifically to increase accessibility to people who otherwise can't because of financial or physical reasons.

Other experiences include:

- **African Safari:** Wild Earth uses a variety of devices to capture some of Africa's most iconic animals.[42] You can interact with an expert game ranger hosting the safari while you watch.
- **The White House:** Google Arts and Culture has filmed a walkthrough the most famous residence in the United States.[43]
- **The Northern Lights:** Lights Over Lapland has a camera pointed north.[44] Commonly seen between November and March, the Northern Lights most commonly appear between 5:00 pm and 2:00 am (UTC +1) and last fifteen to thirty minutes at a time.

42 Wild Earth, *WildEarth,* 2024, wildearth.tv.

43 The White House, "Virtual Tour of the Art and Decor of the White House: The State Floor," *Google Arts & Culture,* artsandculture.google.com/story/jgXBMr-3Z91SjLw.

44 Lights Over Lapland, "Aurora Webcams," *Lights Over Lapland,* lightsoverlapland.com/aurora-webcam.

- **Catacombs of Paris:** The bones of six million people are buried in a complex series of tunnels under Paris.[45]
- **Dive:** My dad was an avid scuba diver and was always a little disappointed that the very idea terrified me. NOAA has created several virtual dives.[46] You might encounter a sea lion, explore the coral reefs of Hawaii, or cave diving in the Channel Island National Marine Sanctuary.

Virtually Visit World-Famous Museums

During the pandemic, more than five hundred museums placed portions of their vast collections online. You might explore Amsterdam's Vincent Van Gogh Museum.[47] Visit Versailles without the crowd getting in the way.[48] Meander through the biggest pile of loot in the world, the British Museum. Study the Tutankhamun Collection at the Egyptian Museum or wander through Seti I's tomb.[49] DuckDuckGo's search engine will bring you hundreds of options for hours of travel without leaving your home.[50]

---

45 Paris Musées, "Virtual Visit," *Les Catacombes De Paris,* Paris Musées, 2025. Available: www.catacombes.paris.fr/en/virtual-visit. Note that, as of time of writing, virtual visits are no longer available, but were during the COVID-19 pandemic.

46 National Ocean Services, "Sanctuaries 360°: Explore the Blue" *National Marine Sanctuaries,* NOAA, Department of Commerce, sanctuaries.noaa.gov/vr/.

47 Van Gogh Museum, Amsterdam, "Enjoy the Museum from Home," Van Gogh Museum, www.vangoghmuseum.nl/en/visit/enjoy-the-museum-from-home.

48 Google, "Palace of Versailles," *Google Arts & Culture,* 2025, g.co/arts/aVz92VH-FAcFfdAGd7

49 The Egyptian Museum, "A Virtual Tour through the Tutankhamun Collection at the Egyptian Museum," Ministry of Antiques: Egypt, 2019, egymonuments.gov.eg/news/a-virtual-tour-through-the-tutankhamun-collection-at-the-egyptian-museum/.

50 *DuckDuckGo,* DuckDuckGo, 2025, duckduckgo.com.

Play Music from Other Cultures

Radio Garden offers live radio all around the world.[51] Just point your mouse at any point on their globe and see what's playing nearby!

Eat the Food of Other Cultures

Whether made by someone else, or tried from a recipe in your own kitchen, you can learn so much about other cultures when enjoying their food. What proteins do they use? How hard are carbs to find. What new spices or ingredients do they take for granted?

Need a reminder of how wonderful the Earth itself is? Watch NASA live streams as they go about their work.[52] Here, you can see watch video feeds of astronauts, rockets, satellites, and the marvelous beauty of our planet.

Where's the Magic?

All this practical stuff is nice and useful, but there are many magic-based things you can do whenever you leave your home.

Carry a Compass

This is classic magic, allowing you a way to find what you need or where to go. Carrying it powers energy for never getting lost.

Keep a Travel Altar in Your Car, Purse, or Backpack

Keeping your tools with you is usually not possible—athames attract attention, after all, and it's rarely a good idea to burn incense in your

51 Radio Garden, "Popular Across the Globe." radio.garden/search.

52 NASA, *Explore NASA+*, 11 Mar. 2025, plus.nasa.gov.

local coffeeshop. Yes, you can work magic, as the old saying goes, naked at high noon in the desert. But I think you'll agree it's always easier—no matter how long you've been practicing—if you've got representations of your personal symbolic language. Putting together a toolkit means you'll always, as the scouts say, be prepared.

I created the first version of the kit I carry now after a work trip that turned out to be super exhausting. My everyday shields were getting spotty, and a lot of random environmental negativity was starting to leak through. A bit of dirt, an old penny, and a fortunate full moon worked the magic I needed. And when I returned home, I decided I didn't want to be so unprepared again. Now I travel with one of three. Each is smaller than 10cm x 5cm (4" by 2") and are easily carried in either my backpack or purse (I don't like my magical tools separated from me, so they don't go into my suitcase, just in case I must check it).

Although the contents of the kits vary slightly, they usually hold:

- **Sticky Notes:** Great for quick petitions and sigils. I use purple because I associate it with magic, but any color or paper would work. (I've done magic using napkins from the cafeteria with a pen borrowed from the front desk.)
- **Incense Holder:** A small pottery piece with a hole in the center holds a stick of incense.
- **Incense Stick** (I like sandalwood) in two pieces.
- **Cotton Embroidery Floss:** Any color will work, as will regular sewing thread. I prefer cotton, as I find silk has magic-dampening properties, and polyester isn't environmentally friendly. This can be used to bind paper petitions, sew sigils, or do knot magic.
- **Cotton Drawstring Bag:** This little beauty is a secret weapon in my traveling magical practice. It can hold herbs to make tea, or a charm. I can sew or draw sigils on it. It can hold special items to tuck into a pocket or for offerings. It folds into a bit of nothing and usually holds the small items in my kit, so they don't rattle around.

- **White Birthday Candle**: This represents the element of Fire, which is sometimes difficult to come by. It burns quickly and cleanly. White is my preference because it covers any magical intent.
- **Pendulum:** Easier to carry around than a deck of Tarot cards, a pendulum is my favorite way to divine while traveling.
- **Penny:** Representing Earth, my penny is old enough to be almost pure copper, which appeals to me. Of course, any stone or bit of dirt will work for this element, but I like the association the penny has with the pentacle on my altar.
- **Safety Pin:** Aside from its potential practical uses, a safety pin can be used to attach notes with sigils to fabric, like the lining of a purse, backpack, or piece of luggage.
- **Sewing Pin:** Needed to sew, it also acts like the safety pin, if a bit more precarious in its hold. Both the safety and sewing pins are made of steel and therefore have beneficial uses when encountering the fae (sometimes I travel with an old-fashioned hat pin).[53]
- **Various Stones:** I have a wide collection of tiny stones that are perfect for magical use. The ones I use most often are a crystal point, turquoise, carnelian, malachite, and citrine.
- **A Wax Paper Packet Containing Useful Herbs:** Most often, I travel with whole cloves, basil, sea salt, or marjoram (see Chapter Two: Correspondences for travel-specific herbs).
- Other items that have come and gone over the years have included a pair of embroidery scissors, a feather, small pencils, and vials of essential oils, water, and salt. If I eat in a food court and can get a packet of salt, I'll often tuck it into my toolkit for the duration of the trip. I don't love that because it so often has iodine in it, but it works.

53 My thanks to Morgan Daimler for that idea.

Create a Vision Board

While I am not a very crafty person, making a vision board is fun, and has proved to be an effective way to manifest my desires. Note that the exact supplies you'll need will depend on exactly what kind of vision board you are making. I usually create the board in my Book of Shadows. Below is a general set of instructions.

You will need:

- Something to attach images to, such as:
  - A blank art book
  - Poster board
  - Large sheet of paper
  - Cork board
  - Index cards
- Something to affix the images, such as glue, clips, or pins
- Writing and drawing utensils, such as markers, pens, or paint
- Images from magazines or other print media, including books
- Scissors
- A large workspace

Before you begin, ask yourself what kind of vision board you want to make and what supplies you need. Consider your intention and what outcome you want. Gather your materials and create sacred space.

With your intention firmly in mind, look for words and images that resonate with that intention and support your dream. If you find images that are close, but not quite what you want, use them to make your own. Trace over images, re-arrange the order of words, use your computer to write new words in fancy fonts and colors.

When you feel like you have all you need, start placing the materials on your board. Don't affix them yet, you want to move things around so that the overall look and feel appeals to you. This may take some time, and I urge you to give yourself permission to step away for a time: have a meal, sleep, do something else. Just remember to create sacred space again when you return.

When you feel the board is as you want it, make it permanent. As you do, put your feelings of contentment, excitement, joy, anticipation—whatever makes sense for you—into the board. You should feel a bit drained when you are finished. Let the board dry a bit.

Put the board somewhere where you can see it, although if you put it in your Book of Shadows (as I do), make a point to look at it frequently. Reconnect with the positive energy you felt while making it.

Draw Sigils

Sigils can be tiny or hidden and they will still work.[54] Some places you might hide sigils include:

- The soles of your shoes
- Inside your shoes
- Under your phone case
- In your wallet
- In your backpack or purse
- On the back of your watch
- On your skin
- In your nail polish
- On your keychain
- On your clothing tags
- On candy wrappers
- On a water bottle label
- In your car (ideas: in the glove box, under a seat, under the floor mats)

Carry a Charm or Talisman

A spell jar doesn't need to be big to pack a lot of power, and it can be charged with "bring to me" energies (charm) or "keep away" energies (talisman), which makes it great for carrying into any uncertain situation.

54 See Chapter Four: Tools for the Journey for a quick look at three ways to work with sigils.

Tiny Spell Jar
You will need:

- A tiny jar with a cork stopper
- Spell components (see below)
- Small candle
- Match

Choose which spell components you want to work with from the list below (more options are in Appendix C):

- **Herbs:** Bay (*Laurus nobilis*), mint (*Mentha*), pepper (including cayenne, *Capsicum annuum*), rosemary (*Salvia rosmarinus*), and thyme (*Thymus vulgaris*).
- **Stones:** Amber, carnelian, citrine, clear quartz, tiger's eye, black tourmaline
- ***Bonus:*** the color of your candle can add to the energy you are creating. I recommend blue for all around calm and safety, red, yellow, or orange for protection, black for warding off negativity, or white for anything. If you have a particular color that resonates with you and what you want the spell jar to manifest, use that.

Hold the jar in your dominant hand (the right hand, for most people) and create a sense of calm within yourself. When you feel ready, tell the jar what you are making, and what its job will be once it's complete.

Fill the jar with the components you gathered. Insert the stopper and light the candle.

Drip the melted wax over the stopper and seal the bottle. As the wax is dripping, repeat your intention. As long as the bottle remains sealed, its potency remains intact.

Plan Your Days Using Magic-Based Timing

Magickal timing is a framework for daily activities and focus based on each day's corresponding energy.

- **Monday (Intention):** Clean your workspace; tidy your desk. List the three (or five) items that must be handled. Plan to finalize or update on Thursday.
- **Tuesday (Movement):** It's an action day: do all the things "out and about" as much as possible.
- **Wednesday (Communication):** Send emails, make calls, hold meetings. Write.
- **Thursday (Finances):** Pay bills, set budgets, review budgets, and finish open tasks.
- **Friday (Creativity):** Celebrate the fun, creative aspects of your life. Spend time with a friend or colleague. Get inspired by current or future projects.
- **Saturday (Planning):** Check your calendar for larger events or longer-term plans; are there any you can take action on? Evaluate ongoing projects and adjust as necessary.
- **Sunday (Relaxation):** Self-care will refill your energy reserves and boost your personal power. Make sure you have quiet time during this day.

Work with a Shamanic Practitioner

Want to visit a place, but know it's practically impossible? Under the direction of a trained shamanic practitioner, you can leave your body behind and visit anywhere in the world. Not all such practitioners do this type of work, so while I know several excellent people doing shamanic work, I can only recommend one: Elizabeth Cashman.

Protect Your Vehicle

I spent most of my working life commuting and I always made a point of giving my car extra protection. Honestly, that didn't completely prevent accidents, but it was never my fault, my insurance always paid top value, and the car was completely repaired or replaced—which, in today's world, seems as if the magic was working. For me, naming my car was a vital part of the protective mechanism. Katy was my zippy 2007 Nissan Sentra. Gus, our beat-up workhouse of a 2006 Subaru Legacy. Nora, our elegant new sedan. Each car's name was chosen for its personality, much like we name our pet. After the car comes into our household and is named, it gets a thorough cleansing—physical and energetic. Incense is lit and smoke wafted into every nook and cranny. Light is shined everywhere, including underneath. The car is praised for its excellence and asked to do a good job protecting on journeys; in return, promises are made to keep it in good working order. It is a partnership. Each Samhain, I would sit in the car, burn incense, and have a talk about how the past year went and what the new year might bring. The partnership would be renewed. Long journeys were often marked by special charm bags tucked into the glove compartment at the outset and removed and deconstructed at the end.

Travel magic takes many forms and does not require expensive or even physical items to work. Sacred travel, whether down the road or around the world, is amazing. It's an enormous privilege to be able to leave the known, the mundane, and explore the rich vast mystery the larger world offers us. When we leave the safe confines of our usual environment, we are given the opportunity to make new connections. When we make new connections, we expand our world and actively experience the diverse gloriousness of what it means to be human. We grow closer to the sacred, linking ourselves to something *more.*

My wish is for you to expand your world through the magic of travel.

Appendix A

General Techniques

Some techniques are common to many spells and charms.

Candle Anointing Technique

All candle work improves if you have time to anoint the candle before you start. To do so, take some olive (or another vegetable) oil on your index and thumb fingers, then stroke the candle, concentrating on the energy or intent you will be working with. If the goal of the working will *attract* or *enhance,* stroke from wick to base (pulling in); if the goal is to *keep away* or *remove,* start with the base and go to the wick (pushing out).

Charging a Charm Bag

Take your bag and pass it over the incense smoke or the candle (carefully) to rid it of unwanted energies. When ready, hold the charm bag and visualize the energy you raised earlier. Will the energy to flow through you and into the bag. When you are done, place the bag between the two candles and let the light from them surround the bag. Let the candles burn down, then go about your day.

Appendix B

All Charms, Divinations, Sachets, Spells, and Talismans in This Volume

Charms

Bag Charm
Braid Charm
Carnelian Charm to Promote Clear Communication
Charm Bag to Avert Anxiety
Charm for Safe Travels
Fast Petition Charms
Fast Sigil Charm for Protection
Mercury Charm Bag
Quick Playing Card Charm
Quick for Car Protection
Rain's End Charm
Snow Charm for Protection
Travel Charm Bag

Divinations

Aid in Decision-Making
Destination Divination
Flower Divination
Pendulum
Stone Divination
Simple Water Divination
Yes/No Playing Card Reading

SACHETS

Safe Travels Sachet
Safe Travels Sachet
Travel Sachet
Vehicle Protection

SPELLS

A Spell to Manifest Travel
A Traveler's Spell
Air Spell
Airplane Spell
Attract Travel into Your life
Break A Mirror Spell
Burning Away Evil Spell
Easy Apple Spell
Energy Boost Spell
For Positive Outlook
Generating a Journey Spell
Ginger Safe Travel Spell
Jupiter Candle Spell
Knot Ladder Travel Spell
Moonstone Travel Spell v1
Moonstone Travel Spell v2
Power of the Stars Spell
Safe Return Binding Spell
Safe Travel Spell
Safe Travel Spell Jar
Simplest Candle Spell
Snow Figure Manifestation Spell
Spell for Safe Return
Successful Travel Bath Spell
Successful Travel Shower Spell
Tarot Card Spell

Travel Safely Spell
Vehicle Protection
Wishing Well

TALISMANS

Travel Talisman
Travel-by-Water Talisman

Appendix C

Spell Jar Components

You will need:

- A small jar with a secure lid or stopper (I often travel with a screw top 5 ml vial to use as an emergency spell bottle)
- Sea salt (ideally, although any salt will do)
- Eggshells rinsed clean of egg
- Items from the lists below. Choose according to your bottle size, what you need, have on hand, and what feels correct

Take three breaths and center yourself. Spend time creating a clear intention for your spell.

Keeping that intention in mind, carefully choose the ingredients you wish to use, thinking about why each one is a part of the spell.[55] For example, you might use cinnamon, marjoram, sandalwood, and fennel to encourage a safe and smooth journey.

Add the ingredients in the order listed above (salt, eggshells, ingredients). When finished, seal the jar.

Courage

- Basil
- Carnelian
- Chives
- Pepper
- Pyrite
- Tiger's eye

55 I suggest you research the ingredients using the information found in Chapter Two: Correspondences.

Communication

- Mint
- Sodalite
- Tiger's eye
- Turquoise

Happiness

- Amethyst
- Cinnamon
- Citrine
- Clear quartz
- Lavender
- Mint
- Rose quartz
- Thyme

Money

- Dill
- Ginger
- Gold
- Malachite
- Moss agate
- Spearmint

Peace

- Silver
- Cumin
- Lavender
- Marjoram
- Violet

Protection

- Amber
- Carnelian
- Citrine
- Frankincense
- Sandalwood
- Success
- Bay leaf
- Clear quartz
- Pyrite
- Rosemary
- Saffron

Travel

- Caraway
- Dill
- Fennel
- Mustard
- Malachite
- Moonstone
- Tiger's eye

Appendix D

Travel Specific Symbols

Airplane
Anchor
Backpack
Beach
Beach bed
Beach Umbrella
Bed
Bicycle
Bird
Boat/Ship
Bus
Camera
Campfire
Car
Compass
Desert
Direction Signpost
Dolphin
Double-decker bus
Film
Flipflops
Foreign flag
Hiker
Horse
Hot Air Balloon
Hotel/Motel
Island
Map
Mountain

Ocean/Sea
Passport
Sandals
Seashore
Shoes/Boots
Skis
Skier
Snorkel Mask/Tank
Suitcase
Sunglasses
Taxi/Cab
Tent
Tickets
Tour bus
Train
Umbrella
Wheel
World/Globe

Glossary

A

Air: One of the four "building blocks" of everything. In many magical traditions, Air corresponds with East, the color yellow, the mind, intelligence, and imagination.

Affirmations: Positive phrases repeated to oneself to manifest specific goals, desires, or experiences.

Altar: A flat surface used for magical workings or religious/spiritual acknowledgment.

Amulet: A magically charged, protective object to deflect or produce specific energies.

Astral Plane: A place generally conceptualized as an invisible parallel world unseen from our solid world of form.

Astrology: The study of and belief in the effects the movements and placements of planets and other heavenly bodies have on the lives and behavior of human beings.

Athame: The knife of the Witch. Although generally pronounced "A-tha-may," the term is of obscure origin, has many variant spellings, and an even greater variety of pronunciations ("Ah-THAM-ee" to rhyme with "whammy"; "ATH-ah-may" or "ah-THAW-may").

Aura: The energy field of the human body, especially that radiant portion visible to psychic vision. The aura can reveal information about an individual's health and emotional state.

B

Banish: The magical act of driving away evil or negativity, sometimes associated with removing spirits.

BCE: "Before Common Era." Synonymous with BC, but without religious bias.

Bodhisattva: A being who has achieved the highest level of enlightenment but delays their entry into Paradise to assist others to enlightenment.

Book of Shadows: A witch's book of rituals, spells, dreams, herbal recipes, magical lore, etc.

C

Cakes and Ale: The sharing of a beverage and food offered to each participant in a ritual or eaten by participants at the end of the ritual as a part of the grounding process.

Call: To invoke Divine and elemental forces.

Cardinal Point: The four directions of North, East, South, and West. Often marked in the circle by candles or other items.

Casting the Circle: The psychic creation of a sphere of energy around the area where a ritual is to be performed, both to concentrate and focus the power raised and to keep out unwanted influences or distractions. The enclosed space exists outside of ordinary space and time.

Cauldron: Representing the womb of the Goddess, it may be three- or four-legged. Most modern practitioners use it either as a symbol, to cook in during a ritual, to burn things in as part of a spell, or for scrying.

CE: "Common Era." Synonymous with AD (*Anno Domini*, "the year of our Lord") but without religious bias.

Centering: The process of moving one's consciousness to one's spiritual center, leading to peace, calmness, strength, clarity, and stability.

Chalice: A ritual tool representing the female principle of creation or the element of Water.

Channeling: A practice wherein you allow a discarnate entity to "borrow" your body to communicate.

Chant: This can be a rhyme, sometimes called a rune, intoned rhythmically to raise power. Such rhymes can be simple and repetitive, making them easier to remember.

Charging: Infusing an object with personal power as an act of magic.

Charm: An amulet or talisman charged and instilled with energy for a specific task.

Circle: Sacred space wherein magic is worked, and ritually raised energy is contained. Also, a gathering of Witches or Pagans (this can get a little confusing: "Our Circle is having a Circle where we will circle in a circle").

Cleansing: The act of removing negative energies from an object or space.

Cone of Power: Psychic energy raised and focused during ritual to achieve a defined purpose.

Conscious Mind: The analytical, materially based, rational half of our consciousness. The part of our mind that is at work while we balance our checkbooks, theorize, communicate, and perform other acts related to the physical world.

Consecrate: To declare or set apart as sacred; to produce the ritual transformation of an item into sacred.

Consecration: 1) A ritual of sanctification or purification. 2) A ritual of dedication. 3) Act of blessing an object or place by instilling it with positive energy for sacred purposes.

Correspondences: A system of symbolic equivalencies used in magic (see also *Magical Correspondences*).

Coven: One name for a group of witches that work together in an organized fashion.

Craft: Short for "Witchcraft" or "the Craft of the Wise." Generally associated with the practical aspects of this spiritual system.

Cross-Quarter Days: Refers to sabbats falling on the solstices or equinoxes.

D

Days of Power: Days triggered by astrological occurrences, moon cycles, or special events—your birthday, your menstrual cycle, your dedication/initiation anniversary, etc. (see also *Sabbat*).

Dedication: In Paganism, a solemn promise or vow made to pursue the path of one's spirituality.

Deity: A god or goddess. Some deities have no gender or fixed form.

Deosil: Clockwise, the direction in which the shadow on a sundial moves as the Sun "moves" across the sky. Opposite of widdershins, moving in this direction symbolizes bringing in life and positive energies.

Divination: The discovery of the unknown through interpreting random patterns or symbols using tools such as clouds, Tarot cards, flames, and smoke. Divination contacts the Psychic Mind by quieting the Conscious Mind through ritual and observation of specific tools. *Divine Power:* The unmanifested, pure energy in a deity; the life force, the ultimate source of all things.

Duality: The opposite of polarity. When used as a religious term, it separates two opposites and places those characteristics into separate god forms.

E

Earth: In many magical traditions, the element corresponds to the North; the colors black, brown, and forest green; and foundation, stability, the human body, all solid material things, and prosperity.

Earthing: Sending excess energy into the Earth. Done in ritual after power has been raised and sent to its goal (see also *Grounding*).

Eclectic: A mixture of beliefs borrowed from various Traditions and Theologies rather than a single Tradition or set of beliefs.

Elements: Usually Earth, Air, Fire, and Water. The building blocks of the universe; everything that exists contains one or more of these energies.

Elementals: Archetypal beings associated with one of the four elements (see also *Quarters*).

Energy: The natural vibration or power we tap into or raise through spells and rituals. Some think of this as something they raise or generate; others that it is always there for the trained person to access.

Equinox: Either of the two times each year, on or about March 21 and September 23, when the Sun crosses the equator; day and night are equal in length.

Evocation: To call something out from within.

F

Fire: In many traditions, the element corresponding to the South, the color red, energy, will, passion, determination, purpose, ambition, and spirituality.

First Quarter: One-half of the Moon appears illuminated by direct sunlight while the illuminated part is increasing. Here, the Moon is associated with the Maiden/Mother aspect of the deity.

Full Moon: The visible Moon is fully illuminated by direct sunlight. Here, the Moon is associated with the Mother aspect of the deity.

G

God: Masculine aspect of deity (see also *Lord*)

Goddess: Feminine aspect of deity (see also *Lady*)

Grounding and Centering: The process of connecting oneself to the Earth (also called grounding) and aligning one's energy flow (also called centering).

Guardians: The beings that protect the four quadrants or elements of the Circle (see also *Quarters*).

H

Hand, Projective: The dominant hand, which emits energy. In dominant left-handed individuals, this will be the left hand. In dominant right-handed individuals, this will be the right hand. If you are ambidextrous but use one hand more than the other, this is your projective hand. If you use both equally, simply choose which hand you would like as your projective hand.

Hand, Receptive: The recessive hand, which receives energy. In dominant left-handed individuals, the receptive hand is the right hand. In dominant right-handed individuals, the receptive hand is the left hand.

Healing: The goal of a great deal of magic, especially among healing-oriented spiritual traditions, is healing.

Heathen: A non-Christian, from "one who dwells on the heath."

Herb: A plant or plant part valued for its medicinal, savory, or aromatic qualities.

Herbalism: The art of using herbs both magically and medicinally to facilitate human needs.

Higher Self: That part of us connecting our corporeal minds to the Collective Unconscious and with the divine knowledge of the universe.

I

Immanence: The belief that divinity exists in all things, including people, and cannot be separated from them.

Incense: Ritual burning of herbs, oils, or other aromatic items to scent the air during acts of magic and ritual to better attune to the goal of the work.

Intuition: A term describing psychic information that unexpectedly reaches the Conscious Mind.

Invocation: To bring something in from without. An appeal or petition to a higher power or powers, such as a deity, usually through prayer. A method of establishing conscious ties with those aspects of a deity that dwell within.

L

Lady: The Goddess; any of the names of Her aspects. She is a triple Goddess—Maiden, Mother, and Crone. She is all-encompassing, containing all creative and procreative properties, all aspects of nurturing and healing, all forms of birth and rebirth, all growth and plenty. All women partake of Her nature and are part of Her, and all things are Her children.

Law of Return: Whatever energy is sent out returns to the sender multiplied. Some traditions say it is multiplied by three and therefore call this principle the "Threefold Law."

Laws of Witchcraft: A list of rules for Witches, focusing on individual conduct and coven operations. They are sometimes called Ordains, and several versions exist. Generally, each coven has a set of Laws, sometimes divided into Spiritual, Physical/Mundane, and Magical categories.

Libation: Ritually given portion of food or drink to a deity, nature spirit, or ghost.

Lord: The God; any of the names of His aspects. He is the Horned God of the Hunt, the Lord of Death and Resurrection, the Laughing Lord. He is the Consort of the Lady, who dies and is reborn yearly. He is sensuality, strength, music, and lust. All men partake of His nature and are part of Him. He is the sun, the sky, and the wind.

Lunar Cycle: A roughly twenty-nine-day cycle during which the visible phase of the Moon waxes from dark to full and wanes to dark again. Much magic is geared to the energies present at certain phases of the cycle.

M

Macrocosm: The world around us.

Magic(k): Using knowledge and focused will to direct energy and manifest a change in physical reality.

Magic Circle: A sphere of personal power extending above and below the ground. In it, one is protected from outside forces while rituals are conducted.

Magical Correspondences: Items, objects, days, colors, moon phases, oils, angels, and herbs used in a ritual or magical working that match the intent or purpose of the celebration or ceremony.

Magical System: The guidelines for interacting with supernatural powers; typically associated with a group. Also called a "tradition."

Maiden: Youngest aspect of the Triple Goddess. She is represented by the waxing moon, as well as the colors white and blue. Her sabbats are Imbolc and Ostara.

Meditation: Reflection, contemplation—turning inward toward the self or outward toward deity or nature. A quiet time in which the practitioner may either dwell upon specific thoughts or symbols or allow them to come unbidden.

Metaphysical: A general term referring to aspects of supernatural reality.

Microcosm: The world in us.

Mind, Conscious: The controlled, intellectual part of the mind that is aware when we are awake; the rational part that thinks.

Mind, Psychic: The subconscious, or unconscious, mind in which we receive psychic impulses. The psychic mind works while we sleep, dream, and meditate.

Monotheism: Belief in one supreme deity with no other forms or aspects.

Mother: The aspect of the Goddess symbolizing motherhood, mid-life, and fertility. She is represented by the full moon, the egg, and the colors red and green. Her sabbats are Midsummer and Lammas.

Myth: Body of lore about any land or people that make up their mythology.

N

Natural Fiber: Cotton (in reference to clothes, bags, etc.), linen (from the flax plant), silk, and wool.

Nontheistic Pagan: A Pagan who works energy and otherwise behaves as a Witch but does not ascribe personification or Godhood to the energy they raise.

O

Occult: Literally, "hidden." Universally applied to a wide range of metaphysical topics outside mainstream theologies. To conceal and hide away knowledge from the uninitiated. From the Latin *occulere.*

P

Pagan: From the Latin *paganus,* meaning "country dweller." One who engages in a spirituality that is not part of the Judo-Christian, Islamic, Hindu, Muslim, Buddhist, or other mainstream religions. All Witches are Pagans, but not all Pagans are Witches.

Pantheon: A collection or group of Gods and Goddesses in a particular religious or mythical structure.

Pantheism: Belief in many deities; Paganism is pantheistic.

Pendulum: A divinatory tool consisting of a device hanging from a string; and the deciphering of its movement. This tool contacts the Psychic Mind.

Plane, mental: The thought process, conscious and unconscious.

Plane, physical: The physical body and its workings through coordination with the mental plane.

Plane, spiritual: A person's perception of life's existence, consisting of belief or lack of belief in the Divine.

Polarity: The concept of equal but opposite energies or powers. For example, goddess/god, night/day, Moon/Sun, birth/death, dark/light, psychic mind/conscious mind.

Polytheism: Belief in the existence of many unrelated deities, each with their dominion and interests, who have no spiritual or familial relationships to one another.

Power, personal: The energies which sustain the body and are used in magic.

Projective Hand: The "dominant" hand through which personal power is sent from the body. Typically, the hand we use for manual activities such as writing, dialing the phone, etc.

Psychic Mind: The subconscious, or unconscious mind, in which we receive psychic impressions. It is at work when we sleep, dream, and meditate. Our direct link with the Divine and with the larger, non-physical world around us.

Q

Quarters: Either the cardinal directions corresponding to the Elements and protected by the Guardians or the sabbats which fall on Equinoxes or Solstices.

R

Rede: "An it harm none, do what thou will."

Ritual: A specific form of movement, manipulation of objects, or inner processes designed to produce specifically intended effects. In religion, ritual is typically geared toward union with the Divine. In magical works, it produces a specific state of consciousness that allows the witch to move energy toward needed goals.

Ritual Tools: General name for magical tools. They vary by tradition and usually represent one of the elements.

Runes: Divination tools, the remnant of ancient Teutonic alphabets. A set of symbols used both in divination and magical work.

S

Sabbat: One of the eight holidays, a time for feasting, partying, and general merrymaking. The word itself has various derivations, but I prefer the argument that it comes from the French *s'ebattre*, which means "to frolic" (see also *Wheel of the Year*).

Scrying: A method of divination. To gaze at or into an object such as a quartz crystal sphere, a pool of water, reflections, or a candle flame while stilling the conscious mind to contact the psychic mind. Scrying allows the scryer to become aware of events before their actual occurrence, as well as to perceive past or present events through other than the five senses.

Secular: Material and worldly as opposed to spiritual; thus, anything not religious.

Self: With a capital "S," a reference to one's entirety of personhood: spirit and soul.

Shrine: A sacred place that holds a collection of objects representing a deity.

Solstice: Occurring twice a year, midway between the two equinoxes, producing a day with the shortest light and longest dark hours in December and a day with the longest light and shortest dark hours in June. Occurs around the twenty-first day of those months.

Spell: A magical ritual, perhaps non-religious, often accompanied by spoken words. A written, spoken, or drawn extension of mental and emotional energy to accomplish a specific goal.

Spiral: This symbol signifies an inward journey, the emergence into consciousness of what was previously hidden. It also suggests the round of seasons, where life unfolds and fades, unfolds again in a repeating cycle.

Spirit: The overall energy that harmoniously powers the universe; the "fifth element."

Sympathetic Magic: The concept of like attracts like; most common way that spells are worked.

T

Taboo: A forbidden object or exercise.

Talisman: An object charged with power to attract a specific force or energy to its bearer.

Tarot: The name given to a specific deck of cards; used as a tool for divinatory purposes. This deck traditionally numbers seventy-eight cards, twenty-one of which are Major Arcana, with the rest divided into the four suits of Minor Arcana.

Telepathy: The act of thought transference.

Tools: The instruments, empowered with magic, used by Pagans in magical and spiritual workings. These include runes, Tarot, candles, crystals, and wands. Tools are cleaned and consecrated before use.

Trance: An altered state of consciousness.

Triple Goddess: One Goddess in all Her three aspects: Maiden, Mother, Crone.

V

Visualization: The process of forming mental images to direct personal power and natural energies for various purposes during magic, including charging and forming the magic circle.

W

Wand: Ritual tool usually representing Fire.

Water: In most magical traditions, this element corresponds with the West, the color blue, the Psychic Mind, intuition, and emotion.

Waxing Crescent: The visible Moon is partly but less than one-half illuminated by direct sunlight while the illuminated part is increasing. The Moon here is Maiden.

Waxing Gibbous: The Moon is more than one-half but not fully illuminated by direct sunlight while the illuminated part increases; three days before the full moon.

Waxing Moon: The phase of the Moon in which the face of the moon is getting larger. The time between a new moon and a full moon.

Wheel of the Year: The full cycle of the eight sabbats in the witches' calendar, occurring at the Equinoxes, Solstices, and on the days marking the midpoints between them. Here is a short list of common names and dates:

Name	**Date**
Yule	Winter Solstice
Imbolc	February 2
Ostara	Spring Equinox
Beltane	April 30
Litha	Summer Solstice
Lammas	August 2
Mabon	Fall Equinox
Samhain	October 31

Widdershins: Counter-clockwise motion, opposite of deosil. Usually used for inward-looking magical purposes or for dispersing negative energies or conditions such as disease.

Witch: Gender-neutral term for a practitioner of the "Craft of the Wise."

Witchcraft: The craft of the Witch. Magic, especially magic utilizing personal power in conjunction with the energies in stones, herbs, colors, and other natural objects.

Witches' Pyramid: A creed and a structure of learning that witches follow: "To Know, To Dare, To Will, and To Be Silent."

References and Resources

There are a few places I specifically found information for travel magic, and those are footnoted throughout the text. Several websites contributed general knowledge about specific deities. However, like many of us who have been exploring alternative spiritualities for a long time, many places have contributed to my knowledge.

Atsma, Aaron J. "Apollon." *Theoi Project*, www.theoi.com/Olympios/Apollon.html.

"Astrodienst – the World's Best Horoscopes." *Astrodienst*, www.astro.com/horoscope.

Atkin, Emily. "Do You Know Where Your Healing Crystals Come From?" *The New Republic*, 11 May 2018, newrepublic.com/article/148190/know-healing-crystals-come-from.

"B Corporation." *B Lab Global*, 2025, www.bcorporation.net.

Bargen, Doris G. "Ancestral to None: Mizuko in Kawabata." *Japanese Journal of Religious Studies*, vol. 19, no. 4, 1992, pp. 337–77, www.jstor.org/stable/30233481.

Beyerl, Paul. *The Master Book of Herbalism.* Phoenix Publishing Inc., 1984.

Blackthorn, Amy. *Blackthorn's Protection Magic: A Witch's Guide to Mental and Physical Self-Defense.* Red Wheel/Weiser Books, 2022.

"Cacao." *New World Encyclopedia*, www.newworldencyclopedia.org/entry/Cacao

Cammann, Schuyler. "Islamic and Indian Magic Squares, Part I." *History of Religions*, vol. 8, no. 3, 1969, pp. 181–209, www.journals.uchicago.edu/doi/abs/10.1086/462584

Cann, Hugh. "Jizo: The patron saint of travellers in Japan." *Inside Japan*, www.insidejapantours.com/blog/2018/07/17/jizo/.

Cartwright, Mark. "Ganesha." *World History Encyclopedia*, 2012 ed.

Clement, Paul A. "A Note on the Thessalian Cult of Enodia." *Hesperia: The Journal of the American School of Classical Studies at Athens*, vol. 8, no. 2, 1939, doi.org/10.2307/146595.

"The Conscious Travel Foundation." *The Conscious Travel Foundation.* ÀNI Private Resorts, Joro Experiences, 2024, www.theconscioustravelfoundation.com.

Conservation International. "Code of Ethics." *Conservation International,* 2025, www.conservation.org/about/our-policies/code-of-ethics%20.

Cotterell, Arthur. *A Dictionary of World Mythology.* Oxford University Press, 1997.

Cunningham, Scott. *The Complete Book of Incense, Oils & Brews.* Llewellyn Publications, 1999.

—. *Cunningham's Encyclopedia of Crystal, Gem & Metal Magic.* Llewellyn Publications, 1988.

—. *Cunningham's Encyclopedia of Magical Herbs.* Llewellyn Publications, 1987.

—. *Magical Herbalism: The Secret Craft of the Wise.* Llewellyn Publications, 1986.

—. *The Complete Book of Incense, Oils & Brews.* Llewellyn Publications, 1995.

De Greef, Kimon. "The White Sage Black Market." *Vice* (24 Aug. 2020): Online. Internet. 28 Oct. 2022. Available: www.vice.com/en/article/m7jkma/the-white-sage-black-market-v27n3.

DuckDuckGo. *DuckDuckGo,* 2025, duckduckgo.com.

Dugan, Ellen. *Book of Witchery: Spells, Charms & Correspondences for Every Day of the Week.* Llewellyn Publications, 2009.

EarthCheck. *EarthCheck.* 2024, earthcheck.org.

Fischer-Rizzi, Susanne. *The Complete Incense Book.* Sterling, 1998.

Garland, Robert. "Ancient Greece: Types of Refugees and Struggles of Resettlement." *Wondrium Daily,* www.wondriumdaily.com/ancient-greece-types-of-refugees-and-struggles-of-resettlement.

Graninger, Charles Denver. "Apollo, Ennodia, and fourth-century Thessaly," *Kernos*, vol. 22, Oct. 2009, doi.org/10.4000/kernos.1775.

—. "The Regional Cults of Thessaly." Dissertation, Cornell University, 2005.

Hagar, Stansbury. "The Celestial Bear." *The Journal of American Folklore*, vol. 13, no. 49, 1900, pp. 92–103. *JSTOR*, doi.org/10.2307/533799.

Hayashi, Takao. "Magic Squares in Indian Mathematics." *Encyclopaedia of the History of Science, Technology, and Medicine in Non-Western Cultures*, second edition. Springer Dordrecht, 2008, pp. 1252–1259.

"Hecate." *New World Encyclopedia*, www.newworldencyclopedia.org/entry/Hecate.

"Hekate." *Theoi Project*, www.theoi.com/Khthonios/Hekate.html.

Hesiod. *Theogony, Works and Days*. Dorothea Wender, translator, Penguin Classics, 1973.

Homer. *The Iliad*. Richard Lattimore, translator. University of Chicago Press, 1951.

Inman, Nick. *A Guide to Mystical France: Secrets, Mysteries, Sacred Sites.* Findhorn, 2016.

"Iris." *Theoi Project*, www.theoi.com/Pontios/Iris.html.

Jordan, Michael. *Encyclopedia of Gods: Over 2,500 Deities of the World.* Facts on File Inc., 1993.

"Khonsu." *Encyclopedia Britannica*, www.britannica.com/topic/Khonsu.

King, Leonard W. *Babylonian Magic and Sorcery: Being, "The Prayers of the Lifting of the Hand."* Luzac and Co., 1896.

Kunimitsu, Kawamura. "Dōsojin." *Encyclopedia of Shinto*, d-museum.kokugakuin.ac.jp/eos/detail/?id=9983.

Kynes, Sandra. *Llewellyn's Complete Book of Correspondences: A Comprehensive and Cross-Referenced Guide for Pagans & Wiccans.* Llewellyn, 2013.

Littleton, C. Scott, editor. *Mythology: The Illustrated Anthology of World Myth and Storytelling.* Duncan Baird, 2002.

Livius, Titus. *History of Rome*, volume 1. George Baker, translator.

Mark, Joshua J. "The Mayan Pantheon: The Many Gods of the Maya." *World History Encyclopedia*, July 2012 edition.

Meehan, Carey. *The Traveller's Guide to Sacred Ireland: A Guide to the Sacred Places of Ireland, Her Legends, Folklore, & People.* Gothic Image, 2002.

"Mercury." *New World Encyclopedia*, www.newworldencyclopedia.org/entry/Mercury_(mythology).

Mili, Maria. "Abstract." *Religion and Society in Ancient Thessaly.* University of Oxford, 2015.

Miller, Stephen G. "The Altar of the Six Goddesses in Thessalian Pherai," *California Studies in Classical Antiquity*, vol. 7, 1974, doi.org/10.2307/25010672.

Monaghan, Patricia. *Encyclopedia of Goddesses and Heroines*. New World Library, 2014.

Muir, Steven. "Blest be the ties that bind—religion on the roads of ancient Greece and Rome." *Travel and Religion in Antiquity*. Philip A. Harland, editor, Wilfred Laurier Press, 2011.

Neal, Carl F. *Incense: Crafting & Use of Magickal Scents*. Llewellyn Publications, 2003.

"Neptune." *Encyclopedia Brittanica*, www.britannica.com/topic/Neptune-Roman-god.

"Neptune." *New World Encyclopedia*, www.newworldencyclopedia.org/entry/Neptune_(mythology).

"Njord." *Encyclopedia Brittanica*, www.britannica.com/topic/Njord.

"Njord." *New World Encyclopedia*, www.newworldencyclopedia.org/entry/Njord.

O'Flaherty, Wendy Doniger. *The Rig Veda: An Anthology*. Penguin, 2000.

Olsen, Brad. *Sacred Places Around the World: 108 Destinations*. CCC Publishing, 2004.

—. *Sacred Places Europe: 108 Destinations*, revised edition. CCC Publishing, 2007.

—. *Sacred Places North America: 108 Destinations*, second edition. CCC Publishing, 2008.

Ovid. *The Metamorphoses*. Horace Gregory, translator. Viking Press, 1958.

Pearson, Nicholas. *Crystal Basics: The Energetic, Healing, and Spiritual Power of 200 Gemstones*. Destiny, 2020.

Pinch, Geraldine. *Handbook of Egyptian Mythology*. ABC-CLIO, 2002.

Pletcher, Kenneth. *The Geography of India: Sacred and Historic Places*. Britannica Educational, 2010.

"Poseidon." *New World Encyclopedia*. www.newworldencyclopedia.org/entry/Poseidon.

Powell, Eric A. "The World of Egyptian Demons," *Archeology Magazine,* May/June 2022, www.archaeology.org/issues/465-2205/features/10481-the-world-of-egyptian-demons.

The Prose Edda. Jesse Byock, translator. Penguin Classics, 2006.

"Poseidon." *Theoi Project,* www.theoi.com/Olympios/Poseidon.html.

The Oxford Guide: Essential Guide to Egyptian Mythology. Donald B. Redford, editor. Berkley, 2003.

Kim, David W., editor. *Sacred Sites and Sacred Stories Across Cultures: Transmission of Oral Tradition, Myth, and Religiosity.* Palgrave MacMillan, 2021.

"Saint Christopher." *Encyclopedia Britannica,* www.britannica.com/biography/Saint-Christopher.

Salicrow. *Path of Elemental Witchcraft: A Wyrd Woman's Book of Shadows.* Destiny, 2022.

Schmandt-Besserat, Denise. "Neolithic Symbolism at 'Ain Ghazal." University of Texas at Austin, Ex Oriente, 2013, dx.doi.org/10.26153/tsw/5879.

Silverstar, Phoenix. *Spells from Scratch: How to Craft Spells that Work.* Llewellyn Publications, 2022.

Simpson, Jacqueline and Steve Roud. *A Dictionary of English Folklore.* Oxford University Press, 2003.

Smith, Jacki. *The Big Book of Candle Magic.* Weiser Books, 2022.

Tate, Karen and Brad Olsen. *Sacred Places of Goddess: 108 Destinations.* CCC Publishing, 2006.

Tearfund. *Tearfund.* "Ethical Practice and Sustainability." The Evangelical Alliance Relief Fund, www.tearfund.org.nz/Ethical-Practice-and-Sustainability.

"Terminus." *Encyclopedia Brittanica,* www.britannica.com/topic/Terminus.

"Terminus." *New World Encyclopedia,* www.newworldencyclopedia.org/entry/Terminus.

Thompson, R. Campbell. "The Devils and Spirits of Babylonia, vol. 1 and 2." *Luzac's Semitic Text and Translation Series,* vol. 14 and 15. Luzac & Co., 1903–1904.

—. *Semitic Magic: Its Origins and Development.* Luzac & Co., 1908.

Traxler, Robert J. and Loa P. *The Ancient Maya.* Stanford University Press, 2006.

United Nations. "Global Code of Ethics for Tourism." *UN Tourism,* United Nations, Aug. 2020. www.unwto.org/background-global-code-ethics-tourism.

—. "Sustainable Development." *UN Tourism,* United Nations, www.unwto.org/sustainable-development.

—. "World Committee on Tourism Ethics." United Nations, www.unwto.org/world-committee-tourism-ethics%20.

United States Environment Programme: Industry and Environment. "Environmental Codes of Conduct for Tourism." UNEP, 1995. digitallibrary.un.org/record/186657?ln=en.

Wegner, Josef. "The Evolution of Ancient Egyptian Seals and Sealing Systems." *Seals and Sealing in the Ancient World: Case Studies from the Near East, Egypt, the Aegean, and South Asia.* Cambridge University Press, 2018.

Whelan, Ed. "Janus—Roman God of Time and Transitions" *Classical Wisdom,* Jan. 2022, classicalwisdom.com/mythology/gods/janus-roman-god-of-time-and-transitions.

WWF. "Values in Action: WWF's Core Standards of Performance." *World Wildlife Fund.* wwf.panda.org/discover/about_wwf/our_values/?.

Yoke, Ho Peng. "Magic Squares in China." *Enclopaedia of the History of Science, Technology, and Medicine in Non-Western Cultures,* second edition. Springer Dordrecht, 2008.

Zakroff, Laura Tempest. *Sigil Witchery: A Witch's Guide to Crafting Magick Symbols.* Llewellyn Publications, 2018.

BIBLIOGRAPHY

Barrett, William. *Psychical Research.* Henry Holt & Co. and Williams and Norgate, 1911.

Cunningham, Scott. *Cunningham's Book of Shadows: The Path of an American Traditionalist.* Llewellyn Publications, 2008.

Deines, Tina. "The Seashell Trade for Souvenirs is Killing Protected Marine Life." *National Geographic* (16 Jul. 2018), www.nationalgeographic.com/animals/article/wildlife-watch-seashells-illegal-trade-handicrafts

Halsted, John. *Godless Paganism: Voices of Non-Theistic Pagans.* Lulu, 2016.

Mancini, Marc. "Where Have All the Seashells Gone?" *Howstuffworks,* 16 Apr. 2024, science.howstuffworks.com/environmental/earth/oceanography/where-have-all-seashells-gone.htm.

Nijman, Vincent. "Souvenirs, Shells, and the Illegal Wildlife Trade." *Journal of Ethnobiology,* vol. 39, no. 2, 4 May 2023. www.researchgate.net/publication/3338265.

Oxford English Dictionary. Oxford University Press, 2023.

Zimmerman, Edith. "I Now Suspect the Vagus Nerve Is the Key to Well-being." *The Cut,* 9 May 2019, www.thecut.com/2019/05/i-now-suspect-the-vagus-nerve-is-the-key-to-well-being.html.